Tales from
"Old Hutch"

The Association for Northern California Historical Research (ANCHR) wishes to thank Dr. James (Jamie) Hutchinson for his help and enthusiastic support in allowing this book to be reprinted by ANCHR. All proceeds from its sale will help ANCHR continue its mission of collecting, preserving, and publishing the history of Northern California.

FRONT COVER

The Main Point of Mull's Concentration Was Never Again to be Caught Off the Job Enough to Hear Voices or Laughter of the Stands

~ William Henry Dethlef Koerner, oil on canvas, 1926
(One of Hutch's favorite western illustrators was "Big Bill" Koerner, as well as Harold Bugbee and Charles Marion Russell)

Association for Northern California Historical Research (ANCHR)
PO Box 3024, Chico, California 95927-3024
(530) 636-0778 • anchr.books@gmail.com • www.anchr.org
Facebook: www.facebook.com/anchrbooks/

Printed by Heidelberg Graphics, Chico, California 95928

Introduction

" Old Hutch," or more formally, William H. Hutchinson (1911-1990) was a master story-teller as all who knew him will testify. A native of Denver, Colorado he acquired a strong interest in the history and the folklore of the American West as he traveled with his father through the Southwest states. To quote from a biographical data sheet prepared by "Hutch" in 1977 he "spent some youthful years as a horse wrangler and would-be cowboy in Arizona; also worked as a fireman, both stationary and locomotive; and mucker in mines, and harvest hand in California, Nevada, and Arizona."

He went to sea from 1933 to 1944, and then served two years ashore in the Labor Relations Department of the Matson Navigation Company. In June 1946 with his wife and two small boys, aged four and two and a half, he settled in the hills of Butte County at Cohasset, well away from the ocean and big companies. His wife had said to him, "You are going to be a writer!"--- and a writer he became, specializing in articles about California and the American West.

In addition to his free-lance writing he wrote, narrated, and produced a series of radio and television programs aired over Chico stations from 1947 to 1954. In 1964 he was invited to join the history Department at Chico State College as a Lecturer on a one-year temporary appointment. He remained a member of the faculty until his retirement in 1978 as a full Professor with Emeritus designation. In 1968 he was recipient of the Distinguished Teacher Award at Chico State, and in 1977 he was honored by the Statewide Academic Senate and the Board of Trustees of the 19-campus California State University by being selected to receive the Outstanding Professor Award, granted annually to just two professors in the statewide system.

"Hutch" was a master wordsmith, possessed with a fantastic memory for the details of history, and with a very extensive, as well as colorful, vocabulary. Accuracy was his guide, and truth was his creed in all his work as teacher and historian.

During the time of his radio and television programs he prepared three books containing stories he had narrated. They were: "A Notebook of the Old West." (1947), "One Man's West" (1948) and "Another Notebook of the Old West" (1954). Each has long been out of print. The Association for Northern California Records and Research (ANCRR) has selected stories from these three books for this present publication. Each story has a Northeastern California attachment. Enjoy them!

Table of Contents

The Naming of Cohasset

"Mountaineers are always free."
—*Classic Motto*

"Yes, and they're generally poor."
—*Farm Advisor*

When you encounter the word *Cohasset* as a California place-name, it brings you up "all standing." It is so entirely unexpected. Like meeting an elderly and dignified Bostonian walking tipsy-toe along the Barbary Coast of yesteryear.

Make no mistake about it; Cohasset is of New England in both word and sound. As New England as baked beans, maple syrup and slate roofs. As New England as codfish balls and the surging, seeking rollers of the Western Ocean that end their march against its rock bound coast. In a State whose place names are usually the liquid syllables of Old Spain or commemoratives of some vanished citizen, Cohasset stands out as the Buttes above the Valley floor.

When the family and I decided that we had had enough of City Life; enough of fog and the Market Street Railway, enough of the steady wages and dry-rot of corporate existence, we bought a property in the foothills—*"El Rancho En Escrow."* Fate ordained that it should be in the district known as Cohasset. We have lived there a year past and have no quarrel with Fate as yet.

Our city friends poorly concealed their belief that we were Hatter-mad to forsake the twin blessings of modern plumbing and cocktail bars. Without fail, they did ask hopefully the location and distance of our new abode: (We think they wanted to compute the driving time and expense from San Francisco but perhaps we do them an injustice.) When we said "*Cohasset,*" most of them said "God Bless You!" and let it go at that. A few, the more erudite, no doubt educated at Harvard or Wellesley, indulged in vast and misdirected speculations as to just how the name made its way from the lobster-pots of Massachusetts to the volcanic ridges of Butte County.

Alas for romance! Cohasset was not named by a homesick Argonaut nostalgic for the shore-dinners of his youth. Neither was it named by a sufferer from hay-fever! The prosaic requirements of Uncle Sam's Postoffice distilled this bit of New England-far-from-home. The district was known as Keefers Ridge in the eighteen sixties. Then it was known as North Point. For almost 60 years now, it has been well and favorably known as . . . you guessed it, didn't you?

In all good feature articles, the metes and bounds of the featured locality are given in detail. Here they are for Cohasset and they may even interest you. They did me.

The School District of Cohasset, this being a taxable or Don't-Be-Delinquent description, comprises most of Sections 23 & 24 North, Range 2 East; and parts of Sections 24 & 25 North, Range 3 East, in the County of Butte.

If this description has failed to produce any

mental images, we offer the following or Fourth Grade version: Cohasset is bounded on the East by Big Chico Creek, on the West by Rock Creek, on the South by Bidwell Park and on the North by the Butte-Tehama County Lines. On paper, it looks like a piece of pie that the waitress cut in a hurry with the point slightly anti-godlin. It is a fair and lovely country. Mostly vertical.

The recorded history of Cohasset goes back into the 1850's. It was then as now a source of lumber for the valley and coastal settlements. Timber, logging and milling have been its destiny ever since Stratton's Mill was erected at the head of Mud Creek about 1862.

As I write this testimonial, I can look longingly out my window through the oaks and see the head-rig foundation, rusting boiler shell and enormous sawdust pile that were left by an enterprise belonging to the turn of the century.

The Keefer family had their pinery and mill in Cohasset for many years. They built their own road, to the north and west of the present road, and fought off Indians to bring the clear sugar pine down the mountain. Many of the houses in Chico that you read about with wonder, wonder because they have lasted for sixty and seventy years, were built of Cohasset Pine.

As we said just previously, the first road that could masquerade under the title was built by the Keefer's in self-defense. They had to get that lumber down the mountain. The present *Via Dolorosa* up the ridge to Cohasset was built in the early part of this century. Built by a potent mixtures of a little County money and lots of free labor donated by the taxpaying residents of the district. The telephone line to Cohasset was built and is still owned and maintained by the residents. The people who settled Cohasset in the seventies, when homestead land was opened up, were a stout-hearted, independent, breed with a decent regard for their own self-respect and the rights of their fellowman. Their descendants carry the strain down unalloyed.

Ishi, the last of the Mill Creek Indians, roamed the upper reaches of Mud Creek until hunger trapped him behind Charley Ward's slaughter house in Oroville and gave modern science a living link with the Stone Age. Too, there was a buried treasure along Mud Creek once but this is a story all its own. Cohasset is quite a place.

Along with the timber it produced, Cohasset exported leading citizens. Witness Martin Polk, muleback mail carrier in his youth, kindly gentleman and Dean of Assessors to-day. A man who knows values . . . those of property and those by which men live. Witness Harry Hume, City Manager of Chico. Witness Bruce Gibson of Standard Oil whose nephew was my shipmate in bygone years. The timber and the people will "do to take along."

They raise apples in Cohasset. Apples that were good enough to take Second Prize at the World's Fair of 1903 in Saint Louis. Apples that made an interesting commercial experiment pay-off at the turn of the century.

Wells-Fargo and Company traded Cohasset apples in Mexico for oranges and tangerines thus developing a two-way traffic for themselves and, oddly enough, making money for the Cohassetites who participated in the venture.

Orcharding is not a vital part of the economy these days. Still, in the Fall when the purple haze hangs o'er the hills and the Ranger Stations have gone South with the geese, you can find boxes in the grocery stores of Chico with the proud legend—"Cohasset Apples."

They are good Apples! Try them for pleasure . . . and don't think that I own an apple orchard. I do not. It interferes with deer hunting, the collection of rejection slips, and my wife's fishing. Besides, ever since I flunked higher mathematics—the twelve times table—I have cherished a dislike for Newton . . . and apples.

Cohasset has all that any other foothill region can offer barring a Water District such as has Pair-O-Dice. It has the finest views of the Great Valley of Superior California that I have ever seen or hope to see. To me, it has one distinct and outstanding advantage. It does not have the overcrowding that too often passes muster for progress and civilization. There is room to stretch and spit, if such be your pleasure, without shocking the neighbors. This may be a short-lived attraction for the P G & E is a'comin' to Cohasset. Indeed, the holes and the poles for the power line lurk along the ridge. Where power comes, the electric garbage disposal is not far behind and there will be another wave of settlement. I hope it doesn't wash us off our little spur ridge where the pines and firs make faery ring about our house.

Maybe when this happens and the voting strength of the district can be felt at the polls, the roads of Cohasset will lose their peculiar advantages. Their peculiar usefulness in frightening away acquaintances who want to drive up for the week-end . . . or their summer vacation . . . or simply a home-cooked meal.

We have said that the district was known once as North Point. This name was current until 1888 when the residents petitioned their government for a post-office of their very own. They wanted to call it North Point, California. This proved a stumbling block. The stories of official reaction to the requested name vary as to details; they agree on the salient point. The postal authorities delivered themselves of this ukase, not quoted verbatim but in substance:

"Please get another name for your postoffice."

The task of selecting this other name devolved upon two young ladies of the district. Miss Marie Gibson, daughter of a resident family, and Miss Electa Welch, teacher of the school that season. They chose and submitted the name "Cohasset" which they said meant City-of-Pines.

The name was accepted and the school district, the tax rolls, the voting precinct, all took the name of the new postoffice. The name selected and adopted is more apt than most considering the relationship between the timber and the community it supports.

A lot of people have done worse when they named their children.

There is no postoffice in Cohasset now. Mail is delivered to the silvery boxes three times a week by contract carrier from Chico. The official address is "Cohasset Route." It is more soul-satisfying to use the unofficial address, "Cohasset Stage." The word "Stage" seems much more akin to the spirit of the people who first settled along Keefer's Ridge.

There is a story, one no doubt incapable of proof. This story states that the fairest valley in Saint Peter's domain, is reserved for Cohassetites to make them feel at home. Even so, the story goes, they are unhappy. If you would debate this, or other points, with the writer, take a drive up the ridge to Cohasset. I am easy to find. I live on the Vilas Road. That's the name of the road, not its description.

THE OROVILLE HOAX

The brilliant banners of Imperial Spain whipped in the winds of the New World for three hundred years and more before Gabriel Moraga, *teniente,* led his *soldados de cueros* up a broad valley to a river that he named in honor of the Holy Sacrament. Then, swinging on up the valley to the west and north, Moraga encountered another river, near the mouth of Stony Creek to-day, to which he gave the name *Jesus Maria.*

The rivers kept these names for a long decade until Luis Antonio Arguello, *capitan,* brother of the ill-starred Concepcion, led a more ambitious expedition up this same valley. When he came to the river named Sacramento by Moraga, *El Capitan* noted the numerous feathers of water fowl that floated on its surface. He renamed this river, *El Rio de las Plumas,* and when he came on up the valley to the river that Moraga had named for Our Saviour and His Mother, Arguello again exercised the privileges of rank and renamed it, too . . . . *Sacramento.* The rivers bear these names to-day.

It is these three centuries, and more as men measure time, between Columbus at Watling's Island and Arguello in the Central Valley that perhaps explain many things. Among them, the curious fashion of our literature, and our more formal histories, to decry the Spaniard in the New World.

15

For these three centuries and more, Spain held the richest portions of the New World in fee lucrative by right of daring. The Spanish "got thar fustest" and the English, the French and the Dutch took what was left. Therefore, it is as acceptable to preach the gospel that the Spaniard was actuated by three motives—Gold Greed Glory—as it is convenient to forget that the Anglo-Saxon held his Bible in one hand and a quit-claim deed in the other whenever he saw lands to his own liking. It is not amiss to assert boldly that the Spaniard deserved to lose his possessions to the northern hordes. After all, was he not an indolent fellow who sat idly on his superb *serape* while somebody else did his sweating for him? These may be all comforting shibboleths but they are a far cry from simple Justice.

The Spaniard of the Great Conquest, from *hidalgo* in shining armor to common soldier in leather jacket, not forgetting the robed and sandalled Padre, was a hard doer and a hard dier as the occasion demanded. Barring horse and armor, offset by mobility and terrain, the Spanish ordnance was not so superior to that of the aborigines they faced as might comfortably be supposed from this distance. It was on a relatively equal footing with the opposition that the Spaniard blazed his trails and left his bones, his bridle-bits and his bastards throughout the land we call the West when the West was very very young.

The Spanish names sound down the years with the heart warming ring of flint lance on steel, of shod hoof on *malpais*. They are names like Cortez and Coronado, Anza and Juan de Onate, Kino and Marcos de Niza, Garces and Junipero Serra. There is, too, the limitless legion with the name *Don Fulano de Tal*, John Doe.

Among these brave Spanish names stands that of Alvar Nunez Cabeza de Vaca, the head of the cow. His name is distinctive and in case it seems typically Spanish, let it stand here that it seems no more odd than such commonly accepted names as Fast or Stout, or BideWell or Broadwater, or even Iron Striker, Eisenhower. The Cow's Head holds another distinction in our heritage besides his name. He made a journey.

Cabeza de Vaca was a *Hijo de Algo,* a Son of a Some One, when he joined the expedition of Pamphilio de Narvaez to explore the lands of Florida. Like the rest of the expedition, de Vaca sweat inside his armor and cursed the mosquitos with round Spanish oaths for some two hundred miles of swampy, steaming Florida coast. Like the rest of the expedition, de Vaca was undoubtedly relieved when Narvaez pitched camp at Apalachee Bay to build boats. Boats meant an end to walking. When the crude craft were ready, the men of Narvaez sailed west across the Gulf of Mexico for the recently conquered lands of Mochtezuma.

This took place some ninety years before Plymouth Rock and all went well until November 6, 1528. The fleet of Narvaez was wrecked on the Texas coast, where the Trinity River meets the Gulf, where Galveston now feeds the commerce of the world.

Cabeza de Vaca made it ashore sans weapons, sans armor, sans everything but the wit and the will to live. Three other dripping survivors rallied around him and their names, too, are writ large upon the tablets of survival; *Dorantes, Maldonado* and *Estevan,* a negro slave from Azmoor.

They turned four faces west, four faces towards the sunset, under the leadership of the man named after the head of a cow. They wandered afoot across the hottest, stickin'est, most desolate terrain on the American continent; the country where "to be afoot was to be no man at all." They were prisoners first of one tribe of Indians, then honored guests of another, then prisoners again. They became shamans of the first order and they lived by their wits and they left their blood among captors and hosts alike.

So it was, on a spring morning in 1536, that the sentry atop the wall of a Spanish outpost called Culiacan, on the Gulf of California, rubbed his eyes and sent up a shout. Four rawhide-tough, scarecrows materialized out of the first flat rays of the morning sun and the *entrada* of Cabeza de Vaca had come to its appointed end. No man knows all the distances he covered nor all the deeds he did and even imagination is a poor substitute for this knowledge.

From Cabeza de Vaca came the fruitless quests for the Seven Cities of Cibolo and the first settlement of New Mexico. From Culiacan, his haven after eight years wandering, went Juan Bautista de Anza to blaze the overland trail to California in 1776 and many of those pioneer *Californios* who followed Anza sprang from the lands de Vaca had traversed.

In the fullness of time, the power and the glory that had been Spain in the New World departed and her last colony, California, trickled through the fingers of Mexico. On a hot summer day in a city on the banks of *El Rio de las Plumas,* an inquiring reporter wrote a story. It was a good story, so good in fact that it was reprinted in the "Weekly Butte Record" for August 2, 1879, from the Oroville "Mercury" in which it first appeared:

"While chopping up an oak tree which they had felled for the purpose of obtaining lumber to construct a cabin, James Reynolds and Joe McCarty, two miners working on Middle Fork of Feather River, found in a cavity in the interior of the tree a piece of parchment, 8 x 14 inches, both sides of which were covered with hieroglyphics, as they thought, excepting four figures, viz: 1542.

The gentlemen very properly decided to preserve the parchment which they did until a man who was hunting in that section stopped at their camp and upon being shown the document offered $50.00 for it. The offer was accepted.

We ran across the purchaser, who proved to be F. M. Castronjo of Madrid, Spain, when he reached this city en route to the Bay. He said the characters on the parchment were Spanish letters; that he, being a well educated Spaniard, had experienced no difficulty in deciphering the writing and informed us that it was a condensed history of the wanderings, trials and tribulations of three men named Emanuel Sagosta, Jose Grareljos and Sebastian Murilo, deserters from the command of Hernando de Soto; that they were, at the time of writing, the sole survivors of a party of thirteen who ran away from the expedition on the 24th of November, 1539, and that this letter was written and put in a knot-hole in the oak on the 29th day of August, 1542; that they were discouraged at the prospect of dying in the wilderness and had no idea as to whither their steps were leading them.

Mr. Castronjo kindly permitted us to look at the parchment which was of a dark cream color, the writing thereon being easily perceived by the naked eye, its color being that of a faded blue.

Prior to leaving this city, Mr. Castronjo had the precious article securely sealed up in a tin can, to keep the air from it, and intends disposing of it to the National Historical Society of Spain. In response to our inquiry, he said the miners told him that the outer edge of the cavity was about five inches within the tree which had grown over and completely closed the hole."

It is still a good story after almost seventy years and it could still serve to fill up space in the "Mercury" that was left open by lack of advertising. It is a story that can be swallowed whole or that can be hotly denied in whole. Best of all, it is a story that can provide a moiety of good idle speculation and in this troubled day and age, such period pieces are few and far between.

For instance, wasn't it providential that the first man to wander into the camp of Reynolds and McCarty should be a "well educated" Spaniard? Wasn't it providential that this Spaniard had the sum of Fifty Dollars, *E Pluribus Spendum,* to exchange for the faded blue hieroglyphics on the dark cream colored parchment? Wasn't it a stroke of luck that the inquiring reporter "ran across" Senor Castronjo and was granted an interview? Wasn't it typical that Jim and Joe needed oak to build their cabin instead of pine or fir or even cedar? And wasn't that parchment a durable piece of animal skin to survive three hundred years and thirty-seven immured in the knot hole of an oak whose sap is a homeopathic remedy for warts? "There are more things in Heaven and Earth, Horatio, than are dreamt of in your philosophy." And yet...... ?

If the parchment was a true reporting, then those three Spaniards made an *entrada* surpassing that of Cabeza de Vaca. At the time of their alleged desertion, the winter of 1539, de Soto was camped around Apalachee Bay, that same Apalachee Bay where Narvaez built his boats a decade earlier. It is a far cry and many years from Apalachee Bay to Culiacan in Mexico as de Vaca made the journey. It is an even longer way and a shorter time from Apalachee Bay to the Middle Fork of Feather River as 'Manuel, Jose and Sebastian wrote it down. If it is a true reporting, then the record of a splendid wayfaring has been lost to our heritage. If it is true, then the Centennial celebrants should ring the changes on this epic with Hollywoodian touches and a fair Indian maiden for the romantic lead.

But.... the parchment cannot be proved; neither can it be disproved to the satisfaction of scholars who acquire reputations and many letters after their names from such matters. The parchment remains a legend and like all legends, it sends out variants, even as the stump of an oak tree sends out new shoots if the tap root be left alive.

One such variant holds that there were only two men who wrote the parchment and that they were not deserters from de Soto's command, but rather soldiers of Hernan Cortez who set out on their own free-booting junket after the conquest of Mexico in 1520. Another story holds that the Indians of the Feather River had a ruling family long before the coming of any white men recorded in the Pioneer Register. This ruling family were of distinctive stature and strength; a family noted for their superior intelligence; a family most distinguished for the lightness of their skin. Perhaps 'Manuel, Jose and Sebastian found refuge and a prop for their declining years in the arms of an early California Pocahontas?

In speculating upon the parchment of 'Manuel, Jose and Sebastian, there is another journey that cannot be overlooked. It is the journey of David Ingram, "sayler," late of Barking, County Essex, Merrie Englande.

Ingram was among those put ashore in October, 1568, from the overburdened English vessel. *Jesus of Lubeck,* John Hawkins, Master. Master Hawkins, a compatriot of Francis Drake and equally adept at extracting Spanish gold from sea water, had a disastrous experience with the "treacherous Dons" at Vera Cruz. When the smoke cleared away, Master Hawkins had one ship of his fleet afloat and too many survivors aboard her for comfort or safety. Wherefor, Master Hawkins put one hundred and fourteen men ashore on the Gulf Coast about thirty miles north of Tampico, Mexico. Most of these men turned south to be seized by the Inquisition as "heretics" and to gain immortality in the pages of "Westward Ho."

Of the twenty men who turned north, only David Ingram, Richard Browne and Richard Twide survived, and this they did by walking across country until they came to the province of New Brunswick at the eastern extremity of Canada. They managed this feat in a scant twelve months and found succor from a French vessel who carried them home to England where their story quickly fell into disbelief . . . saylers' yarns having the same currency then as now.

However, in that portion of Valhalla reserved for those who have fared beyond the world's end, Don Alvar Nunez Cabeza de Vaca, *hidalgo* of Spain, would be lacking in true Spanish punctilio if he failed to congratulate David Ingram, AB of England, on the fact that his scoffed at journey had been authenticated, just recently, beyond peradventure.

So, too, the parchment of the oak tree on the Middle Fork of Feather River may become legitimate. But until it does, what did happen to that parchment itself?

Did Senor Castronjo place it in the Museo Naval in Madrid as Julian Dana heard the story? Or did he throw the "precious article securely sealed up in a tin can to keep the air from it" into the nearest Madrid gutter when he found that two hairy American miners had pulled his leg in far away California? And no matter what happened to the parchment, how did James Reynolds and Joe McCarty spend Senor Castronjo's fifty dollars . . . if they got them?

24

UNCONQUERED

The mountain men who blazed the overland trails to California held a low opinion of the Indians they encountered beyond the high Sierra wall. They weighed them in the balance against such known adversaries as Blackfoot and Crow, Kiowa and Comanche, Sioux and Cheyenne, and found them sadly lacking in warlike skills. They called them "Diggers," an epithet not a name, and killed them as casually as they stepped on the ants that crawled across their path.

Then came the Argonauts, the most virile and agressive blood in the United States, a hundred thousand strong in one brief year. The most warlike of Indians would have been hard pressed to withstand this concentrated impact; the first Californians were submerged, then wiped away, in the flood tide of gold seekers.

Yet of all the proud Amerinds, from Iroquois to Apache, it was one of these despised people who resisted the white man the longest—for almost 35 years after the haughty Sioux whipped Custer, for almost 25 years after the hot-eyed Geronimo surrendered.

You skirt his country now, as you drive north from Chico along the eastern side of the Sacramento Valley on your way to the wonderlands of Shasta Dam or Lassen National Park. The streams that underpass the highway are only names to the uninitiated—the hard, practical, Anglo-Saxon names bestowed so many years ago. There is Mud Creek and Rock Creek, and Pine Creek and Deer Creek; and when you cross Deer Creek, your eyes lift unbidden to the great snow cone of Lassen Peak thrusting aside its crown of thunderheads.

Then you must forget the irrigation and the smell of green things growing in the valley to your left. Then must you see, *and feel,* only the foothill ridges lifting slowly on your right.

They mark a land of old lava flows; cut and canyoned by the streams that you have crossed. It is a land of manzanita and bull pine and oak along the ridges, the canyons choked with pepperwood trees and poison oak bushes six feet tall and strong in proportion. It is a wild and inhospitable land to this day, and few white men live in it by choice.

When you live in it as I do, you know it for the homeland, the beloved country, of the last Stone Age Man north of the Rio Grande who projected himself into the Twentieth Century. He was the last of his people, the sole survivor of over 60 years of unremitting warfare, and his greatest defeat—and final victory—came not from force of arms but from the white man's love of souvenirs.

Before even the Spanish came to California, the Yahi had been forced away from the fertile valleys along the main rivers, the Pit, the Feather and the Sacramento, by sheer force of numbers. More prolific tribes crowded them into the foothill country that no one else wanted, and the country itself, plus their natural gift for trouble, kept them down to what their country could support.

Only rarely, and then at the risk of pitched battle, did they make forays below the 1000 foot contour into the great central valley to gather grasshoppers and then singe off their wings and dry their bodies against the hunger of winter. They gathered grass-seeds on the foothill ridges and followed the harvest up the slopes of Lassen Peak as the summer ripened the higher elevations. They collected acorns in the fall, and these, together with the salmon that used to throng the Sacramento and its tributaries, formed their mainstay against the starvation that always threatened if spring came late to California.

They caught deer with snares made of cunningly twisted milkweed fibres, and by using skin coverings and skillful bleatings to decoy the game within sure arrow shot. If they found a bear, asleep or denned-up, they ringed him with a circle of fire and arrowed him until he dropped, but such largesse of meat came only rarely. Theirs was ever an economy of survival and the white man tilted the scales against them with the finality of civilization.

The vanguard of white invasion came over the Lassen Trail, the Death Route to California, that ran down the dividing ridge between Deer Creek and Mill Creek. The immigrants had horses and mules and cattle that were more easily killed than deer and just as tasty. Indeed, the Yahi quickly developed the mountain lion's taste for horse and mule meat, and these they killed by choice rather than the gaunted oxen.

When the Lassen Trail was no longer used, the Yahi palate led them down into the valley, where the white man had subdued their native enemies, and they raided the livestock of the outlying ranches. To lose his livestock was enough to make the settler wrathy, but when the Yahi compounded the felony by murdering the white man and his family, it was too much.

It was easy to plan reprisals against these marauders from the hills, but it was another thing to make the plans pay-off. The centuries of oppression by their native enemies had given the Yahi a congenital skill in the fine art of "hit and run away." They could confuse a trail to such good purpose that after twenty-four hours, not even the Yahi who made it could tell where they had been. And they took an ironic joy in switching their pursuers onto the trail of Indians of a different tribal extraction.

Their skill in these attainments was proven beyond peradventure when Bob Anderson, Hi Good, John Breckenridge and others found Yahi sign on the Deer Creek Flats. For two long months they followed it, up the Campbell trail to Deer Creek, across to Mill Creek by way of Graham's crossing where they had to "hang on by their teeth," and on to Battle Creek Meadows where Mineral Lodge stands today. The Yahi led them on, around the base of Lassen Peak, even into Hat Creek canyon, and then the Yahi doubled back over the same route with annoying variations to Deer Creek Flats whence they had started.

One branch of the pursuit struck off on another hot scent across country to Keefer's Ridge, Cohasset of today, and all the way to Forest Ranch. At long last, success seemed in sight for they surprised an Indian camp, with whiskey barrels in plain sight, and made "good" corpses out of most of those they found.

The sweetness of their victory was allayed when they discovered that their victims were Butte Creek Indians; among them the squaw of a white man who kept store at Forest Ranch. It was further embittered when Bob Anderson found that his ranch house and barn had been burned, and five head of cattle butchered by the Yahi at the same time he was engaged in fighting the Maidu tribe by Forest Ranch.

Despite these skills, the Yahi had already been reduced below 300 souls when Ishi was born into his embattled people about 1855. Before the outbreak of the Civil War, he and his people had become a source of revenue to the settlers. A purse of $3000 for their extermination was raised by popular subscription and entrusted to a man named Cohen who kept a store at Mayhew's stage station on Deer Creek. A Yahi scalp was sufficient evidence for payment.

If the settlers missed bagging Yahi, they could always count on killing a grizzly or two and selling their galls to the Chinese herb-doctors for $15 apiece. It was a no-quarter fight on both sides, and Ishi's first years conditioned him against the forces both of Man and Nature; a struggle epitomized by the forty scalps that hung from a poplar tree in front of Hi Good's cabin down in Acorn Hollow.

The Yahi did their best to even the count or get a credit balance, and they killed the white men's women and children just as savagely as the white men killed their families. The three Hickok children were murdered at the foot of Rock Creek Ridge in '62, two girls in their teens and their younger brother. A teamster for Keefer, Thomas Allen, was shot off the top of his load as he made his way down the ridge to the valley with lumber. The countryside boiled with excitement and no Indian, no matter what his tribe, was safe from the general animosity.

The following year. Ishi made his first contact with the whites as the result of the murder of the two Lewis boys, Johnny and Jimmy, on Little Dry Creek, northeast of Oroville, and the providential escape of their sister, Thankful. This raid was further complicated by the theft of horses from Solomon Gore.

The pursuing settlers jumped the Indian camp in the half-light before dawn, and the Yahi lost heavily until they scattered in obedience to the ancient principle that flight is better than fight. The victors ransacked the camp, retrieving property, and when they kicked apart a heap of stolen quilts, a solemn eyed boy about nine years old faced them stoically.

Ishi would have died then and there, "nits breed lice," had not Bob Anderson intervened. Ishi was alive amidst the wrecked *campoodie* when his people returned to cremate their dead and to burn their hair down to the scalp in sign of mourning. It was a rite that Ishi knew well before he died.

The close of the Civil War was the beginning of the end for the Yahi. A fresh influx of settlers poured into the valley, men trained in years of savage warfare along the Missouri borderlands. More and more cattle grazed over the ridges, and sheep and hogs came in to compete with the Yahi and the deer for the grass-seed harvest and the acorn crop. Far away from the Yahi country, great hydraulic monitors "piped" thousands of cubic yards of gravel into the streams of the Mother Lode. The "slickens" that ruined the farmers also clogged the Sacramento and the salmon run fell off along the upper tributaries. Not even the white man's skill at extermination could keep the Yahi population in balance with the diminishing food supply, but Ishi lived and grew wise in the desperate art of survival.

He was among the survivors who refuted the claim that the Yahi had been exterminated in revenge for the killings of Mrs. Workman, Scotch John Banks and Miss Roxana Smith, a lass new come from England to reside with her relatives near Concow. And if Ishi knew the secret of the golden coins, good English sovereigns, that the Yahi plundered from the Workman home, it died with him and the sovereigns are still buried in the wilds of Mill Creek canyon.

Ishi was not among the 30 of his people who died in a cave north of Dye Creek, near Bogard's sheep corral, in 1868, but two years later, he came face to face with the hard facts of Yahi life. His ear lobes were pierced for ornaments, and the septum of his nose held a polished bone except when he had a cold. Then it held a sprig of juniper or bay, which acted as a primitive inhaler. He was in his middle teens, admitted to the status of a man, but there were no marriageable women left. It is very doubtful that Ishi wasted much time bemoaning his celibacy; he didn't have time for the luxury of self-pity. The burden of food-getting for the family band was falling more and more upon his shoulders and with his father's increasing age and feebleness, the tasks of successful leadership devolved upon him.

In this same year, 1870, two of Ishi's sisters were captured by the whites. It seems logical to believe that Ishi followed them until the approach of open country made concealment impossible; then watched them disappear in the heat haze of the valley to end their lives on the reservation of an alien tribe.

Two weeks later, a settler near Acorn Hollow, W. J. Segraves, awakened one night to find Yahi in his front yard. Segraves prepared to sell his life dearly, and was understandably relieved when the men handed him their bows in sign of peace. Since they were too strong for him to unbend, Segraves broke them to make sure that the peace would last, and the gathering spent the remainder of the night debating the formalities of surrender in a *lingua franca* of broken Spanish and pidgin Indian. After a breakfast off Segraves' cattle, provided willingly in this instance, the peace conference suddenly dissolved.

A neighbor of Segraves rode over to weigh himself. When he threw the rope of the steelyard over a convenient limb for this purpose, Ishi and his defenseless people scattered like a covey of foothill quail. Their one gesture of submission to the inevitable came to naught despite the best intentions in the world on both sides.

The following year brought disaster to the remnant of the Yahi. They stole some beef steers in Morgan Valley and failed to cover their tracks properly, so great was their haste to eat. Cowboys used dogs to find their hiding place in a cave under the overhanging banks of Mill Creek and they killed all they found, men, women and children. One of the pursuers did boggle at shooting the children with his .56 caliber Spencer rifle: *It tore them up so.* He managed to salve his conscience by doing the job with his six-shooter which was only .38 caliber. Once again the word went out that the Yahi were exterminated but the word reckoned without Ishi.

Ishi realized that the only course left open to him and the battered fragment of his people lay in avoiding any form of public attention. He forbade stealing livestock because this provoked pursuit; any use of firearms was abandoned, and the Yahi reverted to bow and arrow, snare and pitfall, root-digging and fish-spearing — the Stone Age customs of their forefathers.

Ishi's only concession to civilization was to steal the empty bottles that surrounded the white man's camps and cabins. The glass fractured more evenly than the best flint and made the finest arrow points he had ever owned.

In the ensuing 40 years, Ishi lost only two of his people to the white man. In 1878, Rafe Johnson, a good mountain cowboy riding the ridges for stock, flushed two squaws out of an oak thicket. Johnson shook out a loop, roped them both and took them in to civilization.

Ishi had one chance, at least, to even the score ten years later when D. B. Lyon crowded him too closely. Lyon was hunting deer on Antelope Creek when he heard a noise in a buckeye thicket, and crawled in to investigate. He crawled out again with an arrow through his hat, not his heart, and a firm conviction that he was a long way from where he should be hunting deer. Whether it was this incident or just the general pressure of settlement along Mill Creek that prompted the decision, Ishi led his people over the divide from their ancestral haunts into the canyon of Deer Creek to the south, about 1890.

Deer Creek canyon is wild and deep, carved hundreds of feet below the surrounding lava rock, and in a tangle of shrubbery below the mouth of Sulphur Creek, Ishi cunningly concealed his village. Here the remnant of the Yahi made their home while the slow attrition of natural causes, aided perhaps by Elijah Graham's poisoned flour, wore them down until there were but four of them left—Ishi and his immediate family, mother, sister and uncle.

How long these four could have survived must remain conjecture, because in the fall of 1908, a utility company decided to survey the latent power in the rushing water of Deer Creek canyon. A survey crew made headquarters camp below the mouth of Sulphur Creek and started brushing out the proposed flume line down canyon. It was hard, hot, sweaty labor but no different from other such jobs they had done—until the afternoon of November 9, 1908.

Alf Lafferty and Ed Duensing were walking back to camp about dusk this day and as they rounded a bend in the canyon, they saw a naked Indian holding a vicious two-pronged spear. He snarled at them, so they thought, and Alf and Ed "made a crossing of Deer Creek where there hadn't been none before."

The men in camp greeted their story with howls of disbelief.

The work of brushing out next morning had not been long in progress when the men cleared their way squarely into Ishi's last refuge, three small A-shaped shelters of brush and poles, so skillfully concealed that it could not be seen from the outside of the thicket nor from the canyon walls above.

While they were ejaculating over their find, they heard a scrambling noise above them and looked up to see an old man being helped over the rimrock by a middle-aged woman pushing on his buttocks. When they explored the camp, they found an ancient woman huddled beneath a pile of deerskins and canvas scraps in one of the huts. She seemed paralyzed with fright and Jack Apperson brought her a canteen of water and left it beside her.

Then the men helped themselves to whatever took their fancy; fire sticks and arrow flaking tools, a deer snare, the two-pronged fish spear, and such oddments of clothing as struck their fancy, including a cape of wildcat skins. After they had satisfied souvenir hunger, the group went back to work.

By the next morning, consciences had begun to twinge, and they went back to the camp with beads and other mediums of exchange. They were too late! The old woman was gone and the camp was scoured clean of every article they had left behind, although under a pepperwood tree they did find a pile of glass flakings that almost filled a bushel basket—the results of Ishi's arrow making for many years past.

The news of "wild Indians" in Deer Creek canyon prompted a search party very different from any that had sought the Yahi in the past. Dr. T. T. Waterman of the University of California was in charge, and he was prosecuting a matter of great ethnological importance. If these wild Indians were Yahi he could fill a gap in the mosaic of California's aboriginal population. The Yahi had been believed extinct for so long that they were an almost legendary people, and their language, customs and tribal lore were completely unknown. Dr. Waterman and his party were men of good will, but they were too late. Ishi and his people had left the shelter of Deer Creek canyon for the higher, unprotected reaches of the foothills. It was a bitter country in which to wage a winter fight to keep alive, and the odds were all against the last of the Yahi.

When Ishi's camp had been souvenired, it was too late in the year for him to replace his essential tools and weapons before snow flew; he had his bow and arrows, that was all. The food already collected against the winter was safe because it was Yahi practice to conceal their food supply at a distance from their camp so as not to lose everything in a surprise attack. This scanty store became their emergency supply, to be used only when Ishi failed as a hunter, and it was soon exhausted.

The full story of the next three years was never known, but early in their wanderings, the oldest woman and the old man drowned in fording a winter-swollen stream. The next winter, the youngest woman, Ishi's sister, died of pure starvation, and the coyotes ate her body before Ishi had a chance to cremate it. Once again, he hunkered over his fire and singed his hair to the scalp in sign of mourning. For another year, he pursued his lonely search for food, a search that took him farther and farther away from the old Yahi range and led him south and east to the corral of Charley Ward's slaughter-house.

The abbattoir stood outside of Oroville, not too far from town for economical delivery but far enough to avoid offense, and the men who slept there awakened one August morning in 1911 to the sound of excited yelpings outside. A figure crouched in the corral dirt, surrounded by a circle of wary and vociferous dogs.

The figure stood about 5'6", lean and sinewy, with hair burned short to the scalp. His legs were strong and muscular and somehow he gave the impression of a trapped coyote. His fragmentary garment revealed more than it concealed, and around his neck hung a sack containing a few manzanita berries, the Yahi iron rations.

Since all their efforts at conversation proved fruitless, one of the butchers informed Sheriff Webber in Oroville that they had captured a "wild man." They knew he was wild. He couldn't speak English.

When the Sheriff's deputy arrived on the scene, he commandeered a leather butcher's apron and threw it about the "wild man" and took him in custody. The best place to keep him seemed to be the insane cell at the county jail, then unoccupied, and there he was deposited, not without a rough friendliness and a sincere desire to make him comfortable. They overcame the technicality of how to book him properly by calling him "Panama Kid Webber;" combining Constable Toland's nickname with the Sheriff's patronym. When it came to the charge, they were up against it, and he was never charged with anything more offensive than being a wild man.

When the story of his capture gained circulation around Oroville, the "wild man" gained the benefits of the white man's publicity. So many gifts of fruit poured in on him that the Sheriff had to make a public plea for their cessation but not before Ishi had learned that a banana was peeled, a tomato was not peeled, and an orange was. When he sensed that there was nothing worse in store for him than a dry place to sleep and all that even he could possibly eat, Ishi began to take an interest in his new surroundings. This interest was more than reciprocated in the local press and had several startling repercussions.

The Oroville papers played up the story for all they were worth, and the Chico papers stood all the Oroville stories they could take and then retaliated; there was a long standing animosity between the two towns over the proper location of the county seat. The Chico *Record* observed dryly that many nature fakers had secured free meals and fine cigars through the gullibility of newspaper men with space to fill. The Chico *Enterprise* ran an exclusive story stating that Ishi was a true Indian: a half-breed of different extraction had slipped Ishi the grip of the Ancient and Honorable Order of Redmen, and Ishi had come through in style.

Then the story got on the press association wires, and the St. Louis Missouri *Republic* editorialized in these words:

"Here is available material for a stand-pat Presidential candidate. Here is a man . . . . without bias towards the direct primary, whose record is like virgin snow and who has never thought about anything. This last is a qualification of great value. What more could . . . . Uncle Joe (Cannon) ask?"

Besides this favorable publicity, the wire service story brought Ishi to the happiest years of his life and took the Oroville authorities off the unpleasant hook of wondering what to do with him.

All efforts to dispose of their "wild man" to the Bureau of Indian Affairs, to the State or Federal authorities, had been unavailing, and when Dr. T. T. Waterman showed up with a request that the "wild man" be entrusted to the University of California, he was welcomed with open arms.

Dr. Waterman had read the wire service story in the San Francisco papers, compiled a vocabulary of California Indian words, and caught the first train for Oroville. Waterman was playing a hunch that this might be the last of the Yahi, and if he were, the man was certain to be in a completely primitive state, unspoiled by any adoption of or adaptation to the white man's culture. Several of the artifacts souvenired from Deer Creek were brought over and positively identified by Ishi as his own manufacture;

then Bob Anderson came over from Chico and identified the "wild man" as the little boy he had saved from death so many years before.

All these helped, but Waterman got his final confirmation when he was almost at the end of his vocabulary of Indian words. Ishi had shown no signs of recognition as Waterman worked down the list, until Waterman came to the only word he had in Yana dialect, a linguistic cousin to Yahi. The word was *si'win'i,* meaning yellow pine. When Ishi heard it, his face lighted up with pleasure, and he repeated it in his own dialect time and time again. It was the first recognizable human sound he had heard since his sister had died and left him to wander the foothills alone.

The rest of the story is quickly told. As Dr. Waterman and his ward stood on the station platform in Oroville and watched the Western Pacific Limited thunder out of Feather River Canyon and grind slowly to a stop before them, Ishi almost vomited with fright. He had seen trains before but from a great distance, and to him, they were monsters chasing their prey across the valley. He had always concealed himself until they passed out of his sight. He would have bolted for the hills except for the reassuring presence of Dr. Waterman, the man who knew the Yahi word for yellow pine.

The University put him on the payroll as an Assistant Janitor and he was self-suporting until the day he died. More than this, he was able to save something from each paycheck towards his great desire, the purchase of a horse and wagon, to him the acme of worldly possessions.

The name of Ishi, meaning Man, was given him by Waterman after they had reached the stage of intelligible conversation together. His real name could only be spoken by another member of his tribe, never by the bearer himself, so as Ishi he is known to history . . . . and the name is more apt than many bestowed at christenings.

The tall buildings that now surrounded him left Ishi unmoved. They were not nearly so tall as the majestic peaks and crags of his homeland. He was taken to see Harry Fowler start his trans-continental airplane flight, and when the animated birdcage circled above the throng, Waterman told Ishi that a white man was in it. Ishi smiled politely.

Automobiles did not impress him half so much as trolley cars, because trolley cars had a gong to clang and something that went *whoosh* when they started and blew dirt off the tracks. If Ishi could revisit San Francisco today, he would doubtless recognize a few old friends on Market Street.

The most wonderful of all the white man's ways to Ishi were the things we take most for granted— making fire by striking a match, getting water simply by turning a knob and hiding the light with a window shade that disappeared and came again whenever needed. He relished his dry sleeping quarters and revelled in unlimited food from the University cafeteria, but he used tobacco only to humor those friends who gave it to him, and when it came to alcohol, he summed it up succinctly:

"Whisky-tee crazy auna-tee die man."

These were in truth the happiest years of his life— plenty of food, clothing and shelter, friends who were genuinely fond of him for himself, and enough work to keep his hands occupied and his heart strong. He made arrow-heads, the best ones coming from bromo-seltzer bottles and other artifacts which he gave away with a lavish hand. Small boys were instinctively attracted to him, and his working command of the English language reflected their expressions, as when he replied to a kindly lady's query as to whether or not he believed in Jesus by saying "Sure Mike!"

He steadfastly refused to discuss his own family or those last three years of slow starvation, but Ishi was always willing to talk about his people as a tribe. All we know of the Yahi, their customs, legends, music and tribal history came from Ishi—he filled in the gaps of the mosaic.

Ishi believed that "too much wowi" (houses) made so many white men sick. He shared many of our own obsolete superstitions about women and he believed that playing with dogs caused paralysis. His remedy for rattlesnake bite was to split a toad, or large frog, and bind the animal securely to the affected part. He believed that tonsilitis was best cured by blowing ashes down the throat through a hollow cane or quill.

Dr. Saxton Pope, famous physician and archer extraordinary, treated Ishi when he was sick and received implicit confidence and obedience. Pope, you see, was adept at sleight-of-hand tricks, and these Ishi knew and remembered from his boyhood. The Yahi medicine men had also cured disease by plucking bits of thorn and stone, or pieces of down, from the bodies of the afflicted.

It was Dr. Pope who prevailed on Ishi to accompany him on a camping trip back to Deer Creek in the summer of 1914. Pope had to reassure Ishi that they would bring him back to the University, and not abandon him in the wilds, and even then, Pope had to overcome some major objections on the part of the onetime "wild man." Ishi objected to Deer Creek on three main counts:

a) No houses in Deer Creek
b) No beds, tables or chairs in Deer Creek
c) Not enough to eat in Deer Creek.

However, they had a good trip, and Pope comments dryly that Ishi was the only member of the party to bathe every morning in the icy water. Ishi was the best dish-washer in camp, and after his feet toughened up, Pope says he could outwalk any man in the party. This was not unusual, since Pope also recounts that Ishi had the most perfect feet he had ever seen, feet unspoiled by shoes in the pursuit of fashion.

All in all, Ishi adapted himself remarkably to the circumstances that surrounded him, even to the hordes of people that filled the white man's city, and when he died of tuberculosis, he went as he had lived .... without complaint, not railing against the end, with the native dignity he possessed in such great measure.

Dr. Pope and Dr. Waterman, physician and anthropologist, buried him in Olivet Memorial Park in San Francisco after his tribal custom. In his coffin they placed his bow and quiver, some acorn meal, his fire sticks, some dried venison and ten pieces of dentalia, (Yahi money) to see him into the after world. Then the coffin was cremated and the ashes of Ishi and his possessions were placed in an earthenware jar of Indian manufacture and on the outside of the jar was inscribed this legend:

Ishi, the last Yahi Indian, died March 25, 1916.

Niche 601, Room "B," in Olivet Columbarium near San Francisco, is Ishi's—purchased from his savings for a horse and wagon; but his spirit must live on so long as these words of Dr. Waterman remain:

> "He convinced me that there is gentlemanliness which lies outside of all training and is an expression purely of an inward spirit. It has nothing to do with artificially acquired tricks of behavior. Ishi had an innate regard for the other fellow's existence and an inborn considerateness that surpassed in fineness most of the civilized breeding with which I am familiar."

And I look up at a broken arrow-head and a crude stone axe I found in Mud Creek and I wonder if they were not Ishi's and if they were, whether he would approve my ownership.

THE PERDURABLE DANE

On a spring day in 1843, three white men and an
Indian *vaquero* rode steadily down the east bank of
the River of the Holy Sacrament. They drove before
them a horse and a mule repossessed near the red
bluffs from a party of Oregon-bound emigrants whose
sense of property rights had been all-inclusive. As
they came abreast of the Buttes, the *vaquero,* a guide
loaned them by John Sutter, veered to the east to
bring them to that night's destination—Hock Farm
on Feather River.

One of the white men balked at the new direction.
It was his contention that they should continue south
instead of veering off to the east but, since night was
in sight and Hock Farm was still distant, the major-
ity stuck with the Indian guide. The little party separated; two white men following the *vaquero* to Hock
Farm—a hot meal and a good sleep—while the lone
dissenter stuck with his own opinion and went south
until he came to a tule marsh where he spent the night.

Almost a lifetime later, John Bidwell, full of years
and honors, described the aftermath of this incident:

> "Now if you want to see the humor a man
> is in after spending the night in a tule
> marsh full of mosquitos, you ought to have
> seen Peter Lassen when he came to the ranch
> at Hock Farm the next morning. He was
> so mad he would not speak to any of us

45

. . . . and, I think, never forgot or forgave us. Yet, he was a man who had many good .qualities.

He . . . . would do anything and everything necessary (in camp) even to making the coffee, provided those travelling with him would attempt to assist him. If they did not attempt to assist him, they at once became targets of the best style of grumbling that any man born in Denmark is capable of. But of course, each one would attempt to assist and that was all that was necessary to do, for Lassen would drive them away and do it all himself.

Peter Lassen was a very singular man, very industrious, very ingenious and very fond of pioneeering, in fact stubbornly so. He had great confidence in his powers as a woodsman but strangely enough, he always got lost."

When Peter Lassen rode with young John Bidwell in the spring of 1843, he was a man in the vigorous prime of middle-life with the skillful hands and powerful shoulders of a master craftsman in wood and iron. In his veins pulsed the Viking blood that had sailed the serpent-ships beyond the world's end. In his heart coursed the independence of thought and word and deed that have kept Denmark through even the adversity of a civilized era. And on the face of Peter Lassen was his family's mark, "The Lassen Nose."

Behind him as he rode was the memory of early family training and hard farm work. Behind him were six long apprentice years while he learned the

46

blacksmith trade and the peculiarities of good Swedish iron from his uncle, Christian Nilsen. Behind him were four years as a journeyman smith in the shops of others while he prepared himself to start a smithy of his own.

Behind him were the high hopes of that first venture as his own master and behind him was the knowledge that a Dane who had failed in his business was a marked man among his fellow Danes. Behind him, too, were his brother's children who were the first to call him "Uncle Peter" and who had looked to him as to their own father.

Behind him was the long sea voyage to the New World and another start and behind him was the journey from Boston to Keytesville in Missouri. Behind him were eight years of farming and smithing while the yeasty triple forces of the fur trade, the Santa Fe trade and the thunderous pronouncements of Senator Benton worked on him until the legacy of his blood could not be denied and Peter Lassen took the Road to Oregon. Behind him was the overland trek across the face of the continent and a winter in the Wilhammet Valley and behind him was the sea voyage down the coast to California.

Behind him, Peter Lassen emigrant, was the first winter in San Jose where he earned at least twelve *pesos* by repairing a broken musket stock and behind him was the first of his many FIRSTS in California, the first sawmill. Ahead of him stretched a story worthy of the most heroic saga.

In the California of pre-Gold Rush days, and later, he was a notable individual in a society composed entirely of individuals. He was the Harold Ickes of his time, and in this shrewd observation by Henry Lind, there may be the key to the man called "Uncle Peter" by many Indians and Mister "Lawson" by many of his white neighbors.

His life, his character, his deeds and his death, are shrouded in a veil of hearsay. There is an almost total gap in even hearsay knowledge for the eight years he spent in Missouri. If he left any direct evidence of himself, letters, diaries and the like, they must await fortuitous circumstance to make them public. Yet, not even the mist of hearsay can hide the portrait of a very human figure—perhaps the most human of all the pioneers because a later day has not been able, or inclined, to create a prettified image of the man out of his material successes, or the demands of his descendants.

Perhaps the humanness of Peter Lassen is exemplified in the very fact that he left no monuments of legacy to gild his nature and from the evidence at hand, it does not seem that the Danish blacksmith would regret his oversight. He was a man and a Mason who worked with his hands.

The continuing thread of Lassen's singularity spans sixteen years of California history from the Cosumnes River to Honey Lake via Deer Creek and Cache Valley. It is his treatment of Indians.

On the Cosumnes River, an eye-witness recorded the fact that he was "a most extraordinary and industrious man . . . hospitable to everybody also to the Indians who dote on him." Lassen, you see, gave the

Indians half of all the game he killed for packing it into camp for him.

When he settled on Deer Creek, his herds increased and his buildings were built by Indians who were paid for their services. It is no wonder that he could live alone for seven months in the heart of the country claimed by those Indians so unfavorably known to two generations of settlers as the Mill Creeks.

In Cache Valley, he was the man to whom the resident aboriginals turned for leadership in war against the Pit River tribes and for counsel in trade with the emigrants.

In Honey Lake Valley, Peter Lassen negotiated a treaty with the Paiute nation that stands uniquely among all the Indian treaties ever made. This treaty was simplicity itself: any white man found molesting the Paiute lares and penates, including wives, was to be delivered to Lassen and Isaac Roop for judgment; conversely, any Paiute found prowling among the settlers' belongings was to be delivered to Winnemucca for tribal justice. This is a good treaty on paper. It worked so long as Peter Lassen lived.

Lassen's attitude towards Indians becomes even more singular than his eccentric habit of paying them for work performed when you consider that, as late as 1861, California statutes permitted Indians to be indentured, a polite, legalistic weasel-word for slavery, and that as late as 1863, Indians were raided out of the hills and sold in the settlements for servants.

The greatest tribute to Lassen's individual nature rests in the fact that no rumour, not even the jesting gossip that has currency for wit, couples the Dane with misceganation. And this absence of fact or gossip is the more pronounced since he lived for almost twenty years surrounded by opportunities for taking squaws with their own consent.

When Peter Lassen applied for a grant of land, he applied, also, for Mexican citizenship. He had to in order to get the land of his choice, any land, in California. When he became a Mexican citizen, he took on oath of allegiance to the Mexican government,

Wherefor, Lassen marched with Bidwell under the banner of John Sutter in 1845 to support Micheltorena, the duly constituted governor of Alta California, the legal authority of Mexico. Lassen did not receive any extra grants of land for adhering to his oath of allegiance; he asked for nothing extra and it does not seem logical that he expected anything extra. Even if the Lassen mind did not appraise the situation in these moral terms, he had good grounds for his actions. He had worked for Sutter and Bidwell was his friend. If they were for Micheltorena, regardless of motive, then so was Peter Lassen.

Again, when the Bear Flaggers organized themselves to prod Fremont into action, Lassen took no part in this revolt against the country to which he had subscribed his oath. The Bear Flaggers were men known to Lassen; Ide, Merritt, Moon, Ford and others, were his neighbors from the west side of the valley. Fremont was the son-in-law of the man he admired enough to name his townsite, Benton City. Yet, it does not appear upon the records that he took part in the filibustering raid that became legitimate by the grace of formal war with Mexico.

Admittedly, he did not actively oppose the Bear Flaggers in support of his oath of allegiance to Mexico but this lack of action, as well as his lack of support to the revolutionists, may be attributed, if to nothing else, to the fact that he was too busy with his own affairs, building up *Bosquejo Grant*. Politics were a concern of Lassen only when he could see their direct effect on Peter Lassen.

When Lassen rode with Bidwell on that memorable journey up the valley of the Sacramento, the land rolled on and on in broad, broad acres covered with a carpet of wild oat and clover that was belly deep to a horse. It was a land so rich in undisturbed humus that it could mire a saddle blanket after a shower. Game of all kinds literally had to be kicked out of the way; elk and deer ran in droves among the scattered oaks and the bear trails through the willows were as numerous as the sheep trails to water of a later day.

This was the land that Lassen selected for his own, the first grant and the first white habitation north of Marysville. The grant was five square leagues Spanish measure, 22,000 acres more or less, and it lay roughly between the present highway, 99-E, and the Sacramento River along the course of Deer Creek—one league north of the creek and the balance south. Lassen named his grant *Bosquejo*—The Wooded Place—and so long as he built with his hands, it prospered.

The great trouble with *Bosquejo* was its natural resources. The land raised 80 bushels of grain to the acre on first plowing such as it was; Deer Creek had water for power and irrigation; timber was close at hand with a down hill haul and the climate was attractive to anyone accustomed to Missouri. Peter Lassen laid out Benton City, the first townsite north of New Helvetia, and dreamed a dream common to Californians of that day and later.

His dream was comparable to the dream of Sutter but with a difference. Sutter envisioned a great principality in fief to John Sutter, Baron of New Helvetia. Lassen dreamed of a great settlement on Deer Creek but the overtones of Don Pedro Lassen as *haciendado* are lacking. If this concept of Lassen's dream has merit, then his actions assume a certain coherence and his mistakes acquire a reasonable explanation.

Lassen had the ability to see his dream as an overall problem of colonization. Benton City possessed all the natural resources possible but these resources were not fruitful without people to take advantage of them. To get people, you needed a route that would bring them direct to the scene without filtering them through other dreamers farther south. To get people, you needed the cohesive bond of a common culture to make the wilderness less frightening.

These twin needs of people and culture led Peter Lassen eastwards to Missouri in the summer of 1847. He would induce emigrants to take the Lassen Trail direct to Benton City, and he would have the greatest cultural tie then known on the far frontiers—a charter for a Masonic lodge.

Lassen got his charter, the first charter granted a Masonic lodge in California, and in the granting of this charter, his human frailities stand out in clear relief. The charter was issued by the Grand Lodge of Missouri on May 10, 1848, to Western Star Lodge No. 98, Benton City, Upper California, with Sashel Woods as Worshipful Master, Lucien E. Stewart as Senior Warden and Peter Lassen as Junior Warden.

It would seem that the Grand Lodge of Missouri knew that Brother Lassen believed, and actually practiced, the principles of Freemasonry. The issuance of the charter is proof enough. But Lassen's presumed membership in Warren Lodge No. 74, in Keytesville, Missouri, had shown clearly that he was too haphazard in his ritual to be entrusted with the task of separating the sheep from the goats in a new land where the Tyler sometimes patrolled outside the lodge quarters with loaded rifle to prevent unwarranted espionage by inimical, or just overly curious, non-members.

This supposition is supported by the fact that when Lassen left *Bosquejo* for residence in the high Sierra he did not keep up his membership in any lodge. Yet, a goodly number of the men who followed him in search of Gold Lake were men whose names stand on the roll of the forty-four Master Masons who organized the first lodge in San Francisco. Peter Lassen may have been unversed in ritual, he may have been erratic in his dues, but more than most, he practised his creed in his daily life.

The misplaced confidence Lassen held in his ability as a woodsman comes to its fullest flowering in the trail he laid out to California, The Lassen Trail. There is no better example of this confidence than the fact that he induced twelve emigrant wagons to follow him over this cut-off to California before he had ever travelled it himself. There are no better examples of the paradoxes in the character of Peter Lassen than stem from this first journey over the Lassen Trail.

The emigrants threatened to hang Lassen after he led them into some of the damndest country in California. The party almost starved in Big Meadows (Lake Almanor) and reached the valley only by the timely aid of a party of gold seekers coming down from Oregon. Yet, when they did reach the valley at Benton City, after the crowning horror of the Narrows on Deer Creek ridge, Lassen killed his beeves for them. And, after this first-hand acquaintance with the Lassen Trail, Peter Lassen could recommend it two years later as a suitable railroad route across the Sierra.

With a charter for his lodge and an emigrant trail direct to Benton City, Lassen needed one more asset to make his dream come true. He needed a cheap and practical means of transportation with the burgeoning settlement of Sacramento and with the deep-water harbor of Yerba Buena where the tall ships from Boston lay at anchor with the goods of commerce.

The land route down the valley was expensive and even in good weather it was long and wearisome. In wet weather it wasn't jackassable, as Lassen and David Dutton had discovered in 1843 when they camped for two months at the Buttes waiting for the flood waters to recede.

It was this experience, coupled with another experience in 1845 when Lassen, William Moon and Ezekiel Merritt quarried grindstones from a ledge of rock on Stony Creek and floated down the Sacramento peddling their wares clear to the Bay, that led to another first in Lassen's life and his greatest disaster.

His business sense was as misguided as his sense of direction along Pit River but when Lassen had an idea, he prosecuted it with a singlemindedness often mistaken for Danish stubbornness. He bought a shallow draft steam vessel, loaded it with merchandise, and spent five months in the winter of 1849-50 coaxing the vessel up the Sacramento to the mouth of Deer Creek.

The crew, and Lassen, poled the boat when they ran out of fuel, or cordelled it with tow ropes from the bank. They did a variety of tasks not usually associated with travel by water and they ate all the edibles in the cargo to keep alive. While this was going on, passing travellers and others were appropriating the Lassen livestock and the net result of this first steamboat on the upper Sacramento was to bankrupt Lassen beyond repair.

Whether he had embarked upon river navigation with money earned by doing a little placering for gold, or whether it was done solely on the strength of certain promises-to-pay is a matter of conjecture. Lassen came off the river with no money in his purse, which was not unusual, and with a burden of debts for wages, merchandise and the like that had to be paid. Lassen paid them in the only way he knew. He sold his final interest in *Bosquejo,* and it was a respectable holding by even present standards.

His original grant had been somewhat reduced in acreage in 1846, when Lassen deeded all the land north of Deer Creek to Daniel Sill for a consideration that included the provision that Sill would *"help finish a cabin and put a roof on a building on the south side of Deer Creek."* Even in its reduced size, *Bosquejo* looked like a good investment to "General" John Wilson, a disappointed Whig politician from Missouri seeking to better his condition with Federal appointments in California, when he came over the Lassen Trail in 1849.

In addition to his remaining acres, about 18,000 of them, Lassen owned almost 300 head of cattle, most of them "American oxen," 250 fine horses and mules, 200 head of sheep, 500 hogs, twelve wagons, a gristmill, smithy, corrals, cabins and the like. Wilson wrote later that "Uncle Peter Lassen put at me to buy an interest of one-third in his stocked and equipped ranch," which is hard to reconcile with another letter of his in which he speaks of "buying into it the next day after I got into the country and the first California ranch I ever saw." No matter whether Wilson was *put at* to buy an interest, or saw a good thing and grabbed it, the fact remains that the terms of sale were generous.

For a one-third interest in Lassen's stocked and equipped ranch, Wilson agreed to invest the sum of Fifteen Thousand dollars, payable without interest in five years, on January 1, 1855. These terms may be explained by the assumption that Wilson, or his relations, had known Lassen in Missouri. The Wilsons were a prominent clan in Howard County, next door to Keytesville, and this assumption is supported by Wilson's use of "Uncle Peter" as an appellation.

Whatever else "General" Wilson may have been or done, he knew good land when he saw it. He wrote a friend in Missouri about *Bosquejo*: "In agricultural capacity, our soil .... is entirely beyond all you know."

At the same time he sold an interest to Wilson, Lassen sold an equal interest to Joel Palmer who had been in the party of Oregonians that rescued the first emigrants over the Lassen Trail in '48 and who showed up again as the guide to the Wilson wagon train. Palmer's association with *Bosquejo* was of short duration and his entire connection with the project seems obscure.

Lassen's debts from steamboating were not so obscure and since his sales to Wilson and Palmer had no chance of being paid for five years, he sold his own third interest in *Bosquejo* to Henry Gerke together with his claims against Wilson and Palmer. Parenthetically, it should be noted that Lassen planted the first grape cuttings on *Bosquejo* in 1846 and from these small beginnings; as Gerke and then Leland Stanford increased them, came the once largest vineyard in the world that gave its name to the town of Vina, on the site of what was to have been Benton City.

A revealing picture of Lassen's personality at this time comes from the diary of an emigrant who was hired to make a survey of the ranch for the partners, Wilson, Palmer and Lassen. He was a trained and competent surveyor and his diary reflects his exasperation with Lassen's insistence that the survey be

57

performed according to Lassen's own ideas on the matter.

There is more than one diary reference to quitting work for the day because he could no longer abide Lassen's insistent arguments and actions. "Honest but ignorant and stubborn" was the surveyors' verdict; yet he records that when Lassen's trunk was robbed of almost $1400.00 in gold by an emigrant he had befriended, Lassen's only thought was not for his own loss but for the people he owed and whom this money would have paid in part. And this same man, after his wranglings with Lassen over surveying, followed Lassen in the search for Gold Lake.

When the Gold Lake excitement infected the raw camps along the Yuba and Feather Rivers, it swept north to Deer Creek and, like *Crazy* Stoddard farther south, Lassen found himself surrounded by a throng who believed in Lassen's ability to find Gold Lake. The men who followed Stoddard threatened to hang him when he failed to deliver the goods—a lake whose shores were strewn with pebbles, rocks and boulders of pure gold. Lassen escaped this threat but an unkind Fate played a more scurvy trick on him than ever she did on Stoddard, and this assumes that Stoddard once actually found the lake of which he glibly prated and could never find again.

For a man who was not a woodsman, Peter Lassen could cover country. He made a base camp in Big Meadows in the middle of summer and by the time snow drove him out of the mountains, he had traversed an arc from the northern slopes of Mt. Shasta to the headwaters of Feather River by way of the

Warner Range, Honey Lake Valley and almost any other spot you care to name in that vicinity. He prospected in vain over a spot that later produced as much as $3000.00 to a single pan of gravel. It was Rich Bar.

The throng who had started out to use Peter Lassen as a free guide to the lake of gold faded by the wayside, but several stuck with him and among them was the man who partnered Lassen, in fact if not on paper, for six long years. His name was Isidore Meyrowitz, a Master Mason from Fulton Lodge No. 198 in Alabama, or so his name stands on the roster of the founders of California Lodge No. 1 in San Francisco.

Meyrowitz apparently kept a store at Monroeville and he is variously described as being a Pole or a Russian or both. No matter what his extraction or antecedents, he was Lassen's worthy partner until the day he died trying to navigate Honey Lake in a homemade boat. The two diverse partners built a cabin in Cache Valley, about three miles north and east of Greenville, Plumas County, and traded with the emigrants who followed the Feather River ridges down to Marysville.

They put in a garden whose produce they sold to all comers at the flat rate of fifteen cents a pound, regardless of kind. Here Peter Lassen set up his emblem of residence, an anvil before the door, and did smithing for the emigrants while Meyrowitz traded for worn-out livestock to be reconditioned on the lush grasses of the mountain valley. The wheel had come full cycle in a scant eight years.

Down on the Cosumnes in 1843, a Swedish traveller, Dr. Sandels, had visited the homestead of Peter Lassen and found an old Hollander keeping house for him. He had found the cows so tame that they came when Lassen pounded his anvil in a certain way and he had found, rarities among rarities, butter and cheese. So eight years later, the Dane and the Pole, blacksmith and merchant, lived their daily lives and were more self-sufficient than their counterparts manage to be to-day.

The creation of Plumas County in 1854 may have had something to do with Lassen's final change of scene. Maybe it was only the old spring fret stirring the blood of a man who had already made a splendid wayfaring. Whatever it was, Lassen and Meyrowitz went over Diamond Mountain prospecting for the gold of fortune.

They found some settlers at the mouth of Susan River, Isaac Roop and others, who traded with the emigrants taking Noble's Road to California. They found, also, some colors at the head of an arm of Honey Lake and they named the spot Elysian Valley. The prospect looked so good that they went back to Cache Valley for an outfit; and if this sounds like an easy journey, you should try it today. It takes a sheepherder with a jeep and plenty of time to make the grade ... and it is a grade.

They were back in the spot they named Elysian Valley by the end of June and after they dug two miles of ditch, they made good wages until the water played out. The returns were nothing startling but good enough to warrant a permanent change of address. They went back to Cache Valley for supplies to see them through the winter, and by October they had again placed the vasty bulk of Diamond Mountain between themselves and the Plumas County tax assessor and all his works.

Peter Lassen was well past the accepted prime of life but before the deep snows actually settled in, he cut twenty tons of meadow hay to carry his horses through the winter, built a log cabin fifty feet by sixteen feet by seven logs high and roofed it with shakes. As if this were not enough, he occupied the winter by splitting 5000 rails for fencing and whipsawing lumber for a placer flume. John Bidwell had not misjudged his industry.

It almost seems as if the Gods smiled on Peter Lassen in the twilight of his life. The placer paid well, not riches but enough that Peter Lassen did not have to blacksmith or odd-job for hire. His anvil and his forge stood in front of his cabin but he did work only for himself or his friends. No man went away hungry from his cabin and in later years, Asa Fairfield would write it down—"In fifty years residence in this county, I never heard an old settler say anything against Peter Lassen or say that he had trouble with anyone." Peter Lassen may have improved his ability to win friends and influence people, but he never lost his ability to step into a good fight against what he considered unnecessary government.

The men of Honey Lake Valley felt that they had no business being a political subdivision of California. The same reasons that had caused the creation of Plumas County out of Butte County, distance and inaccessibility from the seat of county government, applied equally to them. They had no desire to be residents of Honey Lake Township in the County of Plumas, neither did they relish the prospect of being in Utah Territory under "the Theocratic domination of the Mormon Church."

The step they took was perfectly logical to men of their time, training and temperament. On April 26, 1856, they formed the Territory of Nataqua—P. Lassen, President, I. Roop, Secretary, of the meeting. They set up their own code of laws and established their boundaries. They did a large job in a short time and for some seven years thereafter, the Honey Lakers pursued their conviction that the land east of the Sierra summit had no earthly connection with California. They wound up with Lassen County, still in California by political boundaries.

Long before this theory of geopolitics came to the ultimate conclusion of shots fired with malice aforethought, Peter Lassen had come to the last heat in the forge. It may or may not seem symbolic that the Lassen Trail had a hand in the death of the man who laid it out.

Peter Lassen escaped hanging from the first emigrants who used his *Death Route to California*. He survived the harsh words and threats that were used by those who took it in '49 and '50. But . . . . he could not escape the fascination of a story that came out of it long years later.

James Allen Hardin, a fragment in the tide of '49, had elected to take the Lassen cut-off to the land of gold. Somewhere in the Black Rock Desert of northwestern Nevada, Hardin strayed from the trail and found curious slabs and lumps and chunks of rock scattered about the surface of the ground. He pocketed some of these curious items and when he finally won through to California, and settled around Petaluma, the business of earning a living pushed all thoughts of his curious rocks to the back of his mind.

When he finally got around to having one of them assayed, the years had slid by in single file and it was not until 1858 that Hardin came to Susanville with a party of fellow-seekers to outfit for the Black Rock Desert. The assay of the curious rocks had shown them to be fabulously rich in silver.

Hardin and his companions prospected in vain that year but news of their purpose got around the Honey Lake country. The next spring, Peter Lassen got the urge to go prospecting once again. He left Susanville on April 19, 1859, with two companions, bound for the Black Rock country and a rendezvous with another party of four Honey Lakers under Captain Weatherlow.

Less than two weeks later, Lamericus Wyatt, one of Lassen's two companions, rode a bareback horse into Susanville with the news that Lassen and the other man, Clapper, had been killed by Indians in the night.

A party went out from Susanville and buried Peter Lassen in his blankets on the spot where Wyatt had seen him fall from an unknown gun. In November of that same year, a second party went out from Susanville and brought in his body to be re-interred with full Masonic honors on the spot where he had camped the first night that he became the first permanent settler of Honey Lake Valley.

There he rests today, under a scarred yellow pine that towers over the man-made monuments above his grave and the mystery of his death remains just that.

The fatal shot is presumed to have been fired by Indians; yet why would Indians kill the man who was their proven friend? The Paiutes under Winnemucca were not to blame, so if it was indeed Indians, they were the renegades who followed Smoke Creek Sam or wandering Pit River braves who remembered the drubbing Lassen had given them when they tried to steal squaws from Cache Valley in 1851.

If it wasn't Indians, it was white men. Yet, the only white men known to have been in the vicinity of his death when it occurred were men who lived out their lives in the Honey Lake Valley with the consent and approbation of their neighbors. This was not so easy to do in those days when men made their own laws and enforced them personally for what seemed due cause.

If the murderers of Peter Lassen were renegade Indians or white men unknown to history or to folklore, why did they kill two men for nothing? The camp of Peter Lassen was unplundered when the burial party reached it almost three weeks later. If Lassen was not killed for loot, with overtones of revenge, why was he killed?

The only fragment of explanation belongs in that realm of fancy known as folklore, or legend, and Peter Lassen deserves a legend after death.

The legend holds that Peter Lassen owned a crude chart showing the location of Hardin's rich silver mine in the Black Rock Desert.

This might be dismissed in the light of evidence that it took until 1865, six years after Lassen met his death, before anyone found a mine in the Black Rock Desert that was worth incorporating for purposes of selling stock.

The crude map could be classed as an even cruder tale told around the fire at night to pass the time, or to satisfy the human urge to explain the inexplicable. But .... in the old files of the Chico, California *Record,* under the date of July 1, 1887, there is a story that refurbishes the worn and tattered map of Peter Lassen.

The story concerns a man named Green who claimed that he had the veritable map of Peter Lassen—a map that led him, after three years search, to rich quartz in the foothills east of Vina, near the site known locally as Black Rock on Mill Creek. From the ledge thus discovered, Mr. Green had taken over $2000.00 in wire-gold from ore that he crushed in a hand mortar.

His possession of the map was not explained in the newspaper story; whether he ever found any quartz vein on Mill Creek, a lava canyon of ill-repute, is more doubtful than his possession of the map. And yet .... an emigrant of 1850 is responsible for the statement that Peter Lassen once left *Bosquejo* for the foothills and returned within two weeks with specimens of rich gold ore.

So, Peter Lassen has the ultimate accolade of the western pioneer—a lost mine stands in the shadow of his name even as his monuments stand in the shadow of a yellow pine.

And Peter Lassen, the man who left no material legacy, has other accolades for in the words of Dr. J. N. Bowman "No other person in provincial California has left his name on so many political and natural features, other than streets, as Peter Lassen."

Let the roll call of these tributes toll like a sweet bell heard faintly ringing down a far green valley— Lassen National Forest, Lassen Volcanic National Park, Lassen County and Lassen's Ranch. It is a goodly company but the best is yet to come.

When you drive up the valley lands he was the first to settle, lift up your eyes unto the hills and see his noblest monument—*The-Long-High-Mountain-That-Was-Broken-Off,* Lassen Peak, the eternal tribute to a man who had more heart than judgment.

THE LASSEN TRAIL

Unless you wish to acquire topographical quadrangle sheets and other technical tools, take a plain road map of Nevada and California, some oil company maps are better than others for this purpose, and spread it out on the floor or the dining room table. Turn off the radio, take the telephone off the hook and be churlish to neighbors who want a friendly game of gin rummy or a good gossip.

From a point between Mill City and Imlay, Nevada, where Lawson's Meadows are submerged by Rye Patch Reservoir, trace a line west to Antelope

Springs, then still west to Rabbit Hole Springs and then west and northwest to Big Hot Spring, on the west side of Black Rock Mountain at the southern tip of the Black Rock Range.

Note casually that there are deserts and distances in this country and the barren ribs of mountain ranges. Remind yourself to be sparing with the brackish Humboldt water in your barrels and cherish the hope that this will be a substantial cut-off to California over the central overland route.

Then trace a wavering course up the west side of the Black Rock Range until you come to High Rock Canyon. There are names of other emigrants on the smooth rock walls and you might as well place yours beside them in defiance of the big lonesome that surrounds you.

Then drive carefully up the canyon, being easy on your oxen, to a point about three miles south of Massacre Lake. Your course now turns southwest by way of '49 Canyon across Surprise Valley between Upper and Middle Lakes, and your gaunted oxen plod wearily up the west side of the valley and strain to the lift of Fandango (Lassen) Pass.

From the top of the Pass, Goose Lake spreads out below you to give a sudden wild hope that it is the Pacific until you look on west to see the snow-cones of the main range. Then descend to Goose Lake, using ropes or cables, or a Mormon brake to ease the wagon down the steepest pitches.

Rest awhile at Goose Lake to recruit your stock, if preceding trains have left any decent grass, and then yoke up and plod on down the east side of the Lake until you meet the headwaters of Pit River about four miles west of Alturas. Go down the north side of Pit River, cursing the lava rock, until you come to Canby and then cross over to the south side and into Stone Coal Valley. Then ford and re-ford the Pit, chaining the wheels as you slide down the steep banks and double teaming to make the equally abrupt ascents. All of this takes time in a season of the year when time means life itself to emigrants who are haunted by the Donner Party.

The trail winds on along the Pit into Big Valley, near Bieber, then over a horrendous ridge to Pittville, where you turn south along Horse Creek and go up its course into Little Dixie Valley. Then swing west, around the foot of Blacks Mounttain to Beaver Creek and when you are clear of the escarpment, swing south and east, through the wide-spaced ponderosas, to Poison Lake and Pine Creek, passing west of Feather Lake and Norvall Flat, until you cross Robbers Creek. Then run down your southing along Dry Creek into the Big Meadows with the clouds building up over Lawson's Butte, and the purple autumn haze creeping lower and lower down its side, as a reminder that the year is running out.

There was good grass in Big Meadows before it became Lake Almanor and you can recruit your stock, they need it, with a hopeful prayer that they will gain the strength to top the Deer Creek Ridge before snow flies. So you hook up the spans, four if you are lucky, generally less, perhaps your wagon has been sawed in two to make a little two wheeled cart that one animal can pull, if it gets some help from the family.

Then the trail winds west across Big Meadows up the gradual slope that leads through Soldier Meadows to Deer Creek Pass and down the gentle incline to Deer Creek Meadows and then you pitch upwards onto the ridge between Deer Creek and Mill Creek, into the timber stand called Lawson's Pinery. If you are lucky enough to pass the crowning horror of The Narrows, on the Mill Creek side of the ridge, the worst is behind you and the Sacramento Valley lies shimmering in the smoky autumn light—California!

If you know the country, you can appreciate the emigrants perfectly normal desire to hang the man who led them through it. If you can, or care to, figure distances from the Humboldt Turn against the distance of the Carson or Truckee gateways, you will learn that Lassen's Cut-off was three hundred miles more travel to the promised land.

If you stand by the highway at Canby to-day and look west, you can explain the erratic course that Lassen followed by believing what the emigrants believed—that Lassen steered one day by Mt. Shasta and the next day by Lawson's Butte, depending on which one caught his eye when he rolled out of his blankets in the morning.

And with all its drawbacks, remember that the Lassen Trail set out to do what Chambers of Commerce seek to do to-day—attract emigrants and industry direct to the upper Sacramento Valley without losing the best prospects farther south.

And with all its drawbacks, Lassen was not altogether wrong when he recommended his trail for a railway route across the Sierra. Disregarding his detour from the Humboldt to Goose Lake, railway surveys climbed up Susan River to Big Meadows and only the demands of bankers prevented Deer Creek Canyon from giving the upper valley a direct rail link with the east.

And in simple justice to another man much like Peter Lassen, let it stand here that Lassen followed the trail of Jesse Applegate from the Humboldt Turn to Goose Lake, where Applegate's Cut-off went on to Oregon and Lassen blazed his own trail to Benton City.

And to Henry Lind and Wallace Brokenshire and Martin Polk, go sincere apologies for errors and omissions, for specific lacks, in the route of Peter Lassen. It may be that in some sweet day to come, his trail will be accurately marked, thanks to their efforts.

CHRONOLOGY

1800 to 1830   Peter Lassen was born at Farum, Denmark, some fifteen miles from Copenhagen, on October 31, 1800. He spent the early years of his life helping the family farming venture, driving cattle to Copenhagen, and when he was 17 years of age, he was apprenticed to his uncle, Christian Nilsen to learn the blacksmith trade. He completed his apprenticeship after six years and moved to Copenhagen in 1823 where he spent four years working as a journeyman smith. In 1827, he established his own blacksmith shop and failed in this enterprise about the end of summer in 1830.

He applied for a passport to leave the country and sailed for America on October 12, 1830.

1830 to 1839   Lassen is believed to have arrived at Boston in the first week of 1831. After a brief stay, he moved west to St. Louis, Missouri, and shortly thereafter settled near Keytesville, Chariton County.

The next eight years seem to have been spent in farming, with blacksmith work for his neighbors as a sideline. He is said to have formed a militia company among his neighbors, with himself as Captain, possibly for service in the Mormon troubles of 1838 in western Missouri.

In the spring of 1839, he emigrated to Oregon and reached the Willamette Valley about September 21, 1839. He spent the winter of 1839 and the spring of 1840 near present-day Oregon City.

1840   On July 3, 1840, he took passage for California by the American ship *Lausanne,* Josiah Spalding, Master.

Lausanne reached Bodega Bay on July 16, 1840, and after a three-way squabble between Captain Spalding, the Russian commander, and the military representative of General Vallejo, Lassen and some others purchased horses from the Russians and made their way overland to Sutter's Fort.

From Sutters Fort, Lassen went down river to Yerba Buena and thence on to San Jose where he received permission from the Mexican governor to remain in California.

He spent the winter of 1840 and the spring of 1841 in and around San Jose doing odd jobs for hire.

1841 Probably in the summer of this year, Lassen was engaged by Isaac Graham, an ex-mountain man of diverse talents, to construct and operate a sawmill for him.

The mill was the first in California, water-powered, and Lassen was connected with this enterprise until the fall of 1842, cutting a total estimated between forty and fifty thousand board feet. He took his pay from Graham in livestock, mostly mules.

1842 After severing his connection with Isaac Graham, Lassen may have intended to drive his livestock back to Missouri where California mules were in great demand but for reasons that are not clear, he settled instead, on the Cosumnes River, a short distance from Sutter's Fort.

1843 Lassen appears to have worked for Sutter as both carpenter and blacksmith, taking his pay in livestock and pasturing his animals with Sutter's own herds.

He rode with John Bidwell in the spring of this year through the upper Sacramento Valley as far as the red bluffs and selected the land he desired to make his own.

He filed a petition for naturalization as a Mexican citizen with Governor Micheltorena in October of this year and filed a request for a grant to be known as *Bosquejo*—The Wooded Place on Deer Creek.

There is unconfirmed evidence that Lassen made a preliminary settlement at *Bosquejo* as early as November of this year.

It seems established that he, together with David Dutton, started to drive his livestock from the Cosumnes to Deer Creek in December but were caught by heavy rains and had to lay-over at the Buttes until the early months of 1844..

1844   According to Dutton, they arrived at *Bosquejo* late in January or early in February and at once commenced erecting buildings on the north side of Deer Creek.

He was granted letters of naturalization by Micheltorena in July of this year and received his letters of title to *Bosquejo Grant* in December.

1845   Lassen was a member of Sutter's Foreign Legion in support of Micheltorena against the native *Californios.*

He returned to Sutter's Fort from Southern California about April 1, after the discomfiture of Sutter's party, and proceeded on up the valley to his grant.

During the summer of 1845, Lassen built a crude grist-mill on the banks of Deer Creek and, together with William Moon and Ezekiel Merritt, quarried grindstones from a ledge of rock on Stony Creek, across the river from *Bosquejo,* which they peddled down the Sacramento clear to the Bay.

Returning homewards from this venture, he met William B. Ide, newly arrived at Sutter's Fort with a circular saw and a set of mill irons. Lassen induced Ide to emigrate to *Bosquejo* to build a sawmill on shares in return for a cabin and some land.

Lassen followed Ide north after a lapse of several weeks with another emigrant family to settle on his grant and some difficulty seems to have arisen between Lassen and Ide over which family was to have which cabin. Ide moved west across the river although his later relations with Lassen seem to have been friendly.

1846 Lassen planted the land north of Deer Creek to wheat and planted a vineyard on the south side; total acreage about thirty.

It is believed that he laid out the first rough plan of Benton City on the south side of Deer Creek in this year after he had deeded all the land north of Deer Creek to Daniel Sill, who had acted as his overseer during Lassen's absences in 1845.

In the spring of this year, John Charles Fremont, U. S. Army, spent several weeks in and around Lassen's Ranch on his way to and from Oregon. He was furnished supplies and livestock by Lassen and some authorities say that Lassen was one of the escort who took Lt. Gillespie in pursuit of Fremont; Sam Neal and Bill Sigler being the other members of the escort party.

Lassen has not been established as a member of the Bear Flag group; neither has his active participation in the more formal War with Mexico that followed.

1847 Lassen left California on June 30 for Missouri in company with Commodore Robert F. Stockton, USN, and Lt. Archibald Gillespie, USMC, and reached St. Joseph, Missouri, early in November.

1848 The first Masonic charter ever granted to a California Lodge was issued to Lassen and entrusted to him for transportation to Benton City on May 10.

On his way west this summer, Lassen induced twelve emigrant wagons to follow him over the Lassen Trail to California. The party had a difficult passage and might not have reached their destination if they had not been succored in Big Meadows by a party of gold seekers coming down from Oregon. This first wagon train direct to Benton City arrived there on October 31.

1849   Lassen is said to have engaged in placer mining in this year but such activity remains a speculation.

James Allen Hardin took the Lassen Cut-Off to California with repercussions ten years later.

The first Masonic Lodge in California met at Benton City on October 30, of this year, and late in November, "General" John Wilson reached Benton City via the Lassen Trail and more than a few hardships.

Wilson and Joel Palmer each purchased a one-third interest in *Bosquejo* from Lassen at this time on very generous terms.

It was with his placer profits or on the strength of his sale to Wilson and Palmer that Lassen purchased a steamer and essayed the first navigation of the Upper Sacramento in the winter of 1849-50. The consequences to Lassen were disastrous.

1850   The first elections held in the upper valley took place at Lassen's Ranch; Captain J. D. Potts and Col. Charles Wilson, who purchased Palmer's interest in *Bosquejo,* being elected *alcaldes.*

Lassen spent the summer and fall in a futile search for the mythical Gold Lake. In this prospecting junket, he is believed to have named Honey Lake from the sweet exudate growing on the plants there and to have been the first to name Cache Valley, the Indian Valley of Plumas County today.

Lassen probably sold his remaining interest in *Bosquejo,* together with his claims against Wilson, et al, to Henry Gerke in this year although title did not pass to Gerke until 1852.

1851 to 1855   Lassen and Isidore Meyrowitz, who operated a store at Monroeville, spent the summer of 1851 in Cache Valley trading with the emigrants. Their site was about three miles northeast of Greenville and is marked by a monument today.

They returned to the valley for the winter and in 1852, took up permanent residence in Cache Valley. A man named Burton and a man named Felix are said to have been associated with them.

The specific movements of Lassen during this period are not known but the Cache Valley establishment was his headquarters, until the spring of 1855.

1855   A prospecting trip to Honey Lake Valley resulted in a permanent change of residence for Lassen and Meyrowitz, who together with a few others, built a cabin in Elysian Valley, about five miles south of Susanville and three miles west of Janesville.

1856   On April 26, Lassen presided at the mass meeting in Isaac Roop's cabin that resulted in the Territory of Nataqua, independent of Plumas County, the State of California and Utah Territory, all and singular.

Meyrowitz was drowned while trying to navigate Honey Lake in a home-made boat and the first public act of Nataqua Territory was to arrange for the administration of his estate. Lassen was appointed official surveyor for Nataqua Territory and served as such when necessary until he died.

1857   The Nataqua-ites merged their grievances with those of the settlers around Carson Valley and Lassen was a delegate from Honey Lake to the convention at Mormon Station (Genoa), that created the Territory of Sierra Nevada.

1858   James Allen Hardin arrived in Susanville to prosecute his search for the silver slabs he had picked up in the Black Rock Desert ten years previously.

The men of Honey Lake Valley were instrumental in hanging William Combs Edwards and "Lucky Bill" Torrington for the murder of Henry Gordier, but Lassen does not appear in the contemporary accounts of this affair. He may have been prospecting with Hardin although this is pure conjecture.

1859   Lassen left Susanville on April 19, 1859, with two companions, to search for the Lost Hardin Mine. He was killed on the night of April 28 or 29 by mysterious rifle fire and news of his death reached Susanville about May 7 via Lamericus Wyatt, one of his two companions. Lassen was buried where he fell by a party from Susanville about the middle of May and in November of this year, his body was brought into Susanville and re-interred with full Masonic honors.

1862 First monument erected over Lassen's grave on June 24th.

1863 A militia company known as the Lassen Rangers was formed in Red Bluff on May 15th., presumably for home guard duty against Secessionist sympathizers.

1864 The California Legislature created Lassen County, on April 1st.

1866 Sometime during this year, Lassen's cabin at *Bosquejo Grant* on Deer Creek was razed or destroyed. The cabin stood on the south side of Deer Creek, near the present house of Carl Thomsen.

1887 Joseph Lynch, the last survivor of the party who came to Honey Lake with Lassen in 1855, passed away in the cabin he had helped Lassen build and in which he had lived since Lassen's death. His last request was that he be buried by the side of Peter Lassen.

1896 Lassen's cabin at the upper end of Elysian Valley was destroyed by fire.

1905 Lassen National Forest created on June 2nd.

1907   Lassen Peak created a National Monument on May 6th.

1916   Lassen Volcanic National Park created on August 9th.

1917   A second monument erected over Lassen's grave on September 29th.

1929   Lassen Volcanic National Park enlarged to its present size.

1944   Liberty ship, *Peter Lassen,* christened by Mrs. Jean Hersholt on April 8th, at Wilmington, California.

(There is a monument by the side of Highway 99-E, where it hurtles across Deer Creek, topped with the symbols of Lassen's Faith, the Square and Compass. Another monument rears up in Indian Valley, near Greenville in Plumas County. They are worth seeing for yourself and easy of access. The dates of their erection are upon them.)

Madame Blackjack

There was gold in the gravels of Deer Creek, gold in the hills surrounding the community called Caldwell's Upper Store, gold in the streets of the town itself. Miners took out a quart pot of dust, say $6,000.00, for a day's work and called it quits. The camp produced over eight million dollars in its first two years and gold was where you found it.

An irate storekeeper stepped out of his log and canvas emporium one bright morning to find a miner busily engaged in undermining his front porch. The merchant demanded that the operations cease. The miner leaned on his shovel handle and refused. *"There ain't no law sez I can't dig,"* he said. The merchant reached under his apron and produced a long-barrelled pistol saying *"I'll make a law."* The miner refused to appeal the matter to the court of last resort and the streets of Caldwell's Upper Store were safe, albeit they were so crooked and wandering that they seemed to have been laid out by a drunken miner chasing a burro.

Things had changed a little by 1854 when the rolling varnished Concord coach from Sacramento slid down the long grade from Town Talk into the canyon community now called Nevada City. There was still gold aplenty and the population to dig it, but a certain air of settled respectability had come to the community; a church, some brick buildings, an assay office, a Chinatown section, and a school, plus some indefatigable ladies of stubborn character and irreproachable morals.

The stage angled through the crooked streets and rolled to a halt before the Wells Fargo office on Commercial Street, while the thin red dust of the foothills hung lazily in the air behind it.

The passengers debarked, beating the dust from their clothing and went their ways. One of them stepped daintily down into the street and looked around her with dark, snapping eyes, both interested and interesting. Her name on the waybill was Dumont—Madame Eleanore Dumont —but this brief handle did her an injustice. She had more to recommend her to Nevada City's *hombres* than her exotic name, or her distinctive accent.

Firmly plump in all the right places, well dressed, vivacious, with a healthy glowing complexion of olive hue, she titivated the masculine sensibilities of the onlookers. But despite her impact, Madame behaved with irreproachable decorum on her first arrival. Her bags were taken to the leading hotel, where Madame signed the register with a flourish, ate a hearty evening meal with ladylike delicacy and determination and retired for the night, after locking her chamber door as a lady should. If she knew that she was the object of considerable talk that night in the centers of masculine opinion, it probably was no more than she had hoped.

Women were not the rarity in Nevada City that they had been four years earlier, but the ratio of women to men was still about one to seven. The ratio of unattached women to unattached men was somewhat higher, and the ratio of attractive women to homely ones was highest of them all. The new arrival was definitely attractive and Nevada City sought long and earnestly to assign her to her proper category. Things being as they were, she undoubtedly belonged in one of three classifications: She was a dance hall girl with all the connotations of that term, or she was a school-marm which seemed doubtful, or she might be a woman from the States come out to marry a miner who had not been able, or gentleman enough, to meet her when the stage pulled in. No matter which classification fitted her, Nevada City knew how to act and the community liked to have its women properly classified. It prevented embarrassing moments all around, and a man knew where he stood.

A week went by and Nevada City was at a loss to fit Madame Dumont into any of the standard categories. She stuck closely to her hotel room, or to the parlour reserved for ladies, barring an occasional stroll about the town in broadest day. She minded her own business with exceeding zeal, but was polite and courteous to everyone without familiarity. The worst that was said about her was that she dressed too well which meant, probably, that she had more fashionable clothes and more of them than the local sisterhood.

If there was a Monsieur Dumont to give credence to her title of Madame, the little stranger to Nevada City did not mention him, or explain his absence, then or later. She just appeared out of the Sacramento stage as if that vehicle had conjured her out of thin air at the full-blown age of twenty-five.

Nevada City was at a loss to explain her until a notice appeared inviting all interested parties to the grand opening of Madame Dumont's parlor in Broad Street where there would be free champagne for everyone and an opportunity to test their skill at assembling a fistful of cards whose total pips came closer to 21 than did the cards in the hands of Madame Eleanore Dumont. In short, The Madame was opening a *vingt-et-un* game, a blackjack emporium. She was setting up as a professional gambler.

This unseemly news rocked the staid elements of Nevada City like an overdose of jalap. Theirs was a respectable community with no more knife fights, drunkenness and unwarranted homicide than befitted a prosperous mining camp on the Mother Lode. There were gamblers in the town, of course there were, but they were male gamblers which was fitting and proper. Gambling was a man's job and no more dishonest than politics or mining stock promotions. But a lady gambler, a professional lady gambler, why, why, why that was unheard of! The odds against her staying in business longer than one night, maybe two, became five to one against.

On the announced evening, Madame Dumont opened her gambling house and it was a gala affair. A lady gambler was a rarity. An unattached, attractive woman was an even greater rarity. The combination was enticing. Miners for miles around polished up their boots, took a bath, hefted their pokes and stepped lightfoot into Nevada City to see the sight. Madame was charming. The champagne was plentiful and good. And when it came to blackjack, Madame dealt like a veteran *croupier,* paying her losses or raking in her winnings with an equal courtesy. What her take was for the opening night is not a matter of record, but all accounts agree that it was considerable. When business was over for the night, Madame bade all hands a polite *Bonne Chance, Messieurs,* and retired to her hotel room alone.

This was an auspicious start, but the full measure of Madame's success, the full triumph of her personality, is that she stayed in business. The more respectable elements in the town were outraged even more by her success than they had been at the announcement of her opening. But they had nothing to get their teeth in that would lend an odor of sanctity to her expulsion from the town.

Madame operated with suavity and propriety. She dealt the cards honestly, chaffing the winners, consoling the losers and rolling her own cigarettes with a deftness that bespoke much practice. She took an occasional sip of wine, jollied all *zhee boyss* without becoming forward, and maintained perfect and ladylike decorum in every respect. Nevada City, some of it, was reduced to saying that if she were a lady, she wouldn't be running a gambling game. Well, Eleanore Dumont had never claimed to be a lady. She was a gambler and a good one. She was, also, a Frenchwoman with the innate instincts of her people for managing a commercial enterprise with just the right amount of friendliness and no more.

In fact, the only serious threat to her success was one of over-respectability. She was so young, so pretty, so wide-eyed and charming, that her patrons reacted to it alarmingly. There was no over-indulgence in ardent waters with consequent gunsmoke and property destruction. Inveterate smokers, and chewers, felt uncomfortable despite Madame's own tobacco usage. All these unusual examples of proper conduct came from the patrons themselves; Madame scorned to hire bouncers or strong-arm gents to enforce such decorous behaviour. Under less skillful guidance, such goings on might have

84

given her place the cheerfulness of a funeral home and trade would have come once to see the twin rarities and then sought more masculine atmospheres. But whatever else she had done or been before she arrived in Nevada City, Madame Dumont had made an extensive study of the male animal. She possessed in full measure that quality with which women, smart women, handle large groups of men to their own ends while keeping them all at a safe distance.

She could tug gently at a sleeve here, smile coquettishly up into a bearded face there, talk fluently and with a charming accent on any number of polite topics, and in general bring the air of a Parisian *salon* to the higher California foothills. Her business prospered beyond all reckoning.

Miners swore devoutly that they would rather lose their pile to Madame Dumont than to break the bank against any male tinhorn in California, and they meant it. Her clientele was not confined to Nevada City, far from it. The nearby camps of Downieville, Grass Valley, Washington, Rough and Ready and countless others sent delegations to test the delight of losing their money to Madame Dumont. Once they came, they became repeat customers. No other game in Northern California had such constantly full attendance or such an impressed crowd of spectators. If you couldn't lose your own money to The Madame, the next best thing was to watch somebody else lose his rather than go elsewhere. It was this very press of business that sowed the seeds of Madame's downfall; this, and her chosen brand of gambling.

The gambling game called blackjack, twenty-one, or *vingt-et-un* is self-limiting. Hence, her gambling room might be lipping full with miners, all eager to lose their dust, but Madame could deal to only a half-dozen at a time. She could have dealt twenty-four hours a day and still had plenty of customers but that was manifestly impossible. Her profits were large but the untapped potential was even larger. Madame had a canny business head and this money going to waste appalled her. She needed more dealers and a bigger house to bring her volume up to its proper level.

She knew the impossibility of using any more lady gamblers. For one thing, women who would apply for the job would probably be much more interested in getting the miners excited over themselves than over the cards. For another thing, while Nevada City had reconciled itself to The Madame, any more lady gamblers might put a strain on civic hospitality and tolerance. Madame Dumont decided to hire professional male gamblers who could keep the surplus customers occupied in losing to them while they awaited the supreme delight of losing to The Madame herself.

Her choice for assistant receiver of the public monies fell upon a young, handsome and thoroughly experienced gambler named David Tobin. According to contemporary accounts, he possessed the combined powers of an insurance salesman, a chamber of commerce greeter and an electric calculating machine. Madame knew what she wanted in an assistant and she got it, plus a man who could handle the thousand-and-one vexing problems of detailed management. The one-room premises on Broad Street were enlarged and Dave Tobin was installed in the outer room with a select group of assistants who specialized in faro, poker, keno, chuck-a-luck and three-card monte. This outer room separated the men from the ribbon clerks and Madame's inner room was reserved for the heavy spenders, or for those who had made a lucky winning off Dave and the boys.

Business boomed after Tobin was added to the establishment. Even the failure of Adams & Coy, a great banking house in San Francisco, early in 1855 failed to excite the men of Nevada City as it did less fortunate camps in California. After all, they'd been losing to Madame Dumont for so long that a bank failure was nothing to get excited about, nor was it half so enjoyable as the way they preferred to lose their cash. Things might have gone along in this way forever if Dave Tobin had not been inspired to ask for more than he was getting out of the business late in 1855.

Tobin was a gambler and he knew his odds. Madame Dumont could not handle a business like she now enjoyed without him, or someone like him, to handle the details. And Tobin did not think she could or would find another like him. He put it up to Eleanore Dumont, *Madame Blackjack,* with his cards on the table—more money or he left!

Madame may have let her success go to her head. She may have thought that she could handle the business by herself. She may have resented Tobin's attempt to black-jack her out of what she had built up with herself as the main drawing card. Or she may have been stubborn as women sometimes are. She told Dave Tobin that he could expect no greater share of the profits than he already was getting. Maybe she was bluffing when she said it, but Tobin was just gambler enough to call her. He took his share of the profits and departed for New York where he opened a gambling house of his own. After preying on Civil War profiteers and Tammany politicians very successfully, Dave Tobin cashed in his chips for the last time in 1865 and left a snug fortune to his heirs.

The romantic folks who collect love stories have long insisted that when David Tobin called her bluff, Madame Dumont experienced such an attack of that Fury Hell Hath Nothing Like that the joy went out of her life. It might be true but there is nothing, absolutely nothing, in even legend to show that the relations between Eleanore Dumont and David Tobin were ever more than strictly business. And there is nothing of record, or legend, except affirmative evidence as to Madame's great propriety and moral circumspection during her two years in Nevada City. A broken heart is always more appealing than good business sense when it comes to explaining motives, but Eleanore Dumont was a business woman, and a gambler.

As a business woman, she realized that she had skimmed the cream off Nevada City. Also, the placers were playing out in the fall of 1855 and the great deep quartz mines had not yet been fully developed. There was a slow but steady drift of population away from Nevada City in these months which may explain Tobin's willingness to depart and does explain why Eleanore Dumont boarded the outbound stage early in 1856 and left Nevada City as she had arrived.

Where she went and what she did after she left Nevada City does not matter. Out of this span of years come stories that do nothing but dim the glory of her stay in Nevada City, that do nothing but tarnish the unique niche she carved for herself as the West's only truly professional lady gambler. Those two years were her highwater mark, when she separated men from their money and made them like it without giving up anything of her dignity, her youth, her self-respect, or her person. That is more than many know how to do today. So what she did after that halcyon time has no part in this story.

All that matters is a brief item in the Sacramento *Union* for September 9, 1879, datelined from the high, hard camp of Bodie, Nevada: *A woman named Eleanore Dumont was found dead today about one mile out of town having committed suicide.*

She left no explanatory note. She told no one what she was about to do. She had come to the last card in the deck, turned it over, and broken her hand for twenty-one. She walked out into the bleak, sagebrush studded hills around Bodie, took the little bottle she always carried and cashed in her chips. Maybe not a lady first and last, but a gambler all the time.

Free State of Never Sweat

As its Founding Fathers laid it out, *Nataqua Terri-tory* encompassed some fifty thousand square miles that included choice portions of both California and Nevada real estate. This historical heritage is still a matter of general pride to the present inhabitants of that area but now, in Nataqua's once-capital city, the epithet of *"Never Sweat"* can be used with impunity, which was not the case when Nataqua's shots for independence were still clear echoes in men's minds and hearts.

Nataqua had its genesis in a perfectly logical Califor-nia desire—to trade with the travelling public before somebody else did it first. The desire came to public attention because William Noble was an unsuccessful prospector. He went eastwards from *(Old)* Shasta, the great valley freighting center of the 50s, into Honey Lake Valley and beyond seeking Gold Lake or, perhaps, the Lost Hardin Mine of silver slabs atop the alkali. When he returned to Shasta in the fall of '51, quite empty-handed, his listeners commiserated with him. When he mentioned that he had found a very practicable route from the Humboldt River in Nevada to Shasta in Cali-fornia, the local businessmen pricked up their ears and opened their purses.

The overland routes to California then in use de-bouched into the valley too far south, Marysville and Sacramento way, to be of value to Shasta. The merchants of those river towns were not ones to let steady customers get away from their own spheres of influence. A new road—this road of Bill Noble's—would bring emigrants, unmolested and unplucked, direct to the upper Sacra-mento Valley.

Isaac Roop, publican and postmaster of Shasta, led the subscription list to build the road and when spring weather came in '52, Noble and a little band of devotees set forth to swing the tide of empire from its rutted course. Well, after the Donner Party's fate in 1846, after the disasters that befell those who took Peter Lassen's *Death Route* in '49, emigrants were chary of glib strangers beside the trail who prattled of short-cuts to the Promised Land. Noble did succeed in diverting a train of the less sophisticated to his new route. It was thus proven to be eminently practical and the word began to spread.

The next summer, Isaac Roop, himself, went out to trade with the emigrants between the Humboldt Turn and Shasta. Business was brisk, his stock was soon exhausted, and Roop returned to Shasta well-satisfied. So satisfied, in fact, that when fire destroyed his holdings in Shasta that fall of '53, Roop decided to make the new land he had visited his home.

On a bench above the river canyon that took Noble's Road west, up and out of the Honey Lake Valley, Roop built his cabin and made his stand, naming the river, *Susan,* for his daughter back in "the States." His home-site became the nucleus for others who settled there that year—finding that Roop had chosen wisely—that the land thereabouts was rich in unplundered humus and finding, too, that the tourist trade was good that year. Over 9,000 head of livestock, 436 humans and 88 wagons used Noble's Road to California and the unsigned entries in the Roop House Register reflect the temper of the times and the men who wrote them— *"August 16—blacksmith tools damned high. old iron, wagon tires, etc. scarce. why in God's name can't some of the women stop here?"*. But these entries reflected only minor annoyances. The vexing question was What State were they in or, Where was California's Eastern Boundary?

This same question had vexed the constitutional convention at Monterey in 1849. The "large state" faction sought the crest of the Rocky Mountains as the eastern boundary. The "small state" faction were content to settle for the Sierra summit. The small staters had reason on their side but this was not quite enough. Over in Deseret, the Mormons were claiming the Sierra Summit as their western boundary. The hard facts of Sierran

90

geography would thus entitle them to all Southern California as far north as Santa Monica, plus a good half of Kern and Tulare counties, as the Sierra veered to meet the sea. Such a *contretemps* was unthinkable. So the California Constitution called for an eastern boundary of the 120th Meridian from the Oregon line south to its intersection with a northwest line drawn from the point where the 35th Parallel met the turgid waters of the Colorado River.

It was one thing to lay out the 120th Meridian on paper. It was quite another thing to tell where this arbitrament of geography lay on the ground itself. To compound the confusion, the Enabling Act providing for California's admission into the Union called for the line to be *the Sierra summit* from the northwest intersection with the 120th Meridian. No survey, however, seemed necessary for California's actual admission on September 9, 1850, nor for the creation on this same day of Utah Territory, with a western boundary fixed as The State of California, wherever that might be on the face of the land itself.

Because of this confusion and, quite possibly, from another deep-rooted American dislike, the male population, there was no other gender, of the trading center clustered together in Isaac Roop's cabin on April 26, 1856, twenty strong, and struck a blow for liberty. Electing Peter Lassen to preside and Isaac Roop to record the proceedings, they then and there created *Nataqua Territory,* free and independent of both Brigham Young and whomever happened to be Governor in Sacramento at the moment.

They laid out their boundaries with a generous hand; from the Oregon line south along the 120th Meridian to the 39th Parallel; thence east half-way across Nevada (use Belmont for a point), thence north, via Austin and Battle Mountain to the southwest corner of Idaho, thence west to the point of beginning—that ubiquitous Meridian, the 120th, *which they thought conformed to the Sierra summit line.* The name they chose for their new domain reflected the salient lack of their community, for *Nataqua* meant "woman," perhaps "beautiful woman" and there were none of either kind thereabouts. Having defined their territory and given it a name, they decided on simple laws regarding land claims and water rights and adjourned, having done a large job in a short time.

Some valley newspapers carried a brief mention of this sudden eruption of independence but no other California reaction was noticeable at the time, while Brigham Young had bigger troubles, the Federal troops under Albert Sidney Johnston, to occupy his energies. It was not until a year later, when the traffic over Noble's Road hit an all-time high that Plumas County, California, took cognizance of its long neglected, indeed almost forgotten, eastern region—an area as remote as the moon seven months out of the year from the county seat at Quincy, across the snow-clogged bulk of Diamond Mountain. Honey Lake Valley was decreed to be a full-fledged township of Plumas County, especially with regard to taxes.

The Marysville (Calif.) *Express* preserved Nataqua's reaction to this move: "The citizens of Honey Lake are as violently opposed as ever to the exercise of any jurisdiction by Plumas County. There is, however, some little inconsistency in their conduct for when the tax collector of Plumas County came among them they told him they were in Utah and when Orson Hyde had visited them, they said they lived in California."

Coupled with their understandable attitude towards taxes, the men of Nataqua, and by now their women, too, retained their determination to get a state of their own east of the Sierra Nevada where it and they belonged. After Orson Hyde uprooted the Mormon stake in Carson and Washoe Valleys, the Honey Lakers united with the Gentiles of that region to merge Nataqua into the dream of *Sierra Nevada Territory*—"from the NE corner of California east across Nevada thence southeast to a point forty miles north of Phoenix, thence due south to the Mexican line, thence west to the SE corner of California and thence north to the point of beginning along the Sierra summit." To implement this dream, Judge J. M. Crane was sent to Washington as their lobbyist, but this

Territory never came to pass until the impact of the Comstock Lode created Nevada Territory with slightly smaller dimensions.

Now the creation of Nevada Territory looked like the answer to Nataqua's prayer. Susanville, the heart of Nataqua, became the county seat of Roop County, Nevada. County officials were elected and all was organized according to the statutes made and provided, among them, in the Enabling Act for Nevada Territory, being the joker that the western boundary of that Territory was the Sierra summit.

This official action caused an equally official reaction in Plumas County, California. That county refused to recognize the status of Roop County, Nevada Territory. A separate election was held in Susanville for officials of Honey Lake Township, County of Plumas, State of California. The inevitable result was foreshadowed in an entry made in his diary by one of the Plumas-elected JP's: *"Helped Court take some potatoes of Jones. Women was armed with pistols, knives, shovels and clubs. Three women."*

In the middle of February, 1863, an armed posse from Plumas County swapped shots with the men of Nataqua, forted in Isaac Roop's cabin. There were no fatalities—the men on each side knew one another well enough to know that a pulled trigger meant "meat in the pot" if wanted—but there were wounded on both sides who shed their blood to good purpose. Out of this Sagebrush War came the completion of the actual survey of California's eastern boundary in the summer and fall of '63. There are die-hards in the Great Basin to this day who maintain they were euchered because a Native Son's father ran the line by the California Constitution, that 120th Meridian, rather than by the Sierra summit. This survey showed conclusively that Susanville and the Honey Lake Valley were part of California and, having thus lost the battle, the men of Nataqua proceeded to win the war by getting their own county created, thus solving their difficulty with Plumas, and again launching themselves upon the sea of self-government.

Lassen County was large, it still is, but the original population was even smaller than now. A high tax rate, self-inflicted, was so inadequate that one citizen who received a county warrant for a week's jury duty traded it for a pair of halters and figured he came out ahead. Traffic over Noble's Road, as well as the once lucrative sale of Honey Lake crops to the Comstock mines, both were vanishing under the encroachment of the Central Pacific across the Sierra. Things looked bleak for the county coffers until a rash of mining camps erupted in the southwestern corner of Idaho.

To supply these camps, John Bidwell built a toll road from his chosen city of Chico in the Sacramento Valley over the Humboldt Grade to Susanville whence a road led across northwestern Nevada to Silver City, Ruby City, Boise and Owyhee in Idaho. As many as fifty freight teams a day went over this road in addition to a tri-weekly stage—"It tried to go up one week and tried to come back the next." What this meant to Lassen County was pungently expressed by Messrs. Forbes and Perkins, who ran a newspaper in Unionville, Nevada:

"Honey Lakers, for the purpose of more effectively preying upon the rest of the world, got up a county organization last year. They had no legitimate revenue to conduct a county government and they knew it. But they have tax collectors and these lie in wait for teams passing to and from the Humboldt and come upon the teamsters for taxes on their property. *Civilized men fare better passing among Indians!*" And from the outraged purses of the wagonmasters came this final blast in the columns of the *Humboldt Register:* "Never Sweats is the trite sobriquet given to the people of Honey Lake Valley. It is so easy to get a living there that people acquire indolent habits we suppose."

Today, one of the loveliest roads in California, State Highway 36, can lead you eastwards from Red Bluff across the high plateau country to a sign that says Lassen County. For all comfortable purposes, this sign stands where Noble's Road and the Humboldt Road joined. The highway goes on, paralleling the older roads, to top Fredonyer Pass, named for Dr. Atlas Fredonyer who was expelled from Nataqua for the high crime of Plumasism. The road drops swiftly then to Susanville, standing as ever on the benchland above Susan River and there, still standing, is Isaac Roop's log cabin—the capitol building of Nataqua, the Fort Defiance of the Sagebrush War, a preserved monument to the spirit that turned *Nataqua Territory* into their own local government.

CRAZY STODDART'S SEARCH

Two things there were that helped men's minds and hearts and souls gulp down the tale of "Crazy" Stoddart; one was a legend, the other, a group of facts.

The legend was older than the New World of which it was a part. It was the myth of *El Dorado,* The Gilded Man, the fabled chieftain who anointed himself with dust of gold and washed it away into a sacred lake to propitiate his Gods. It was this tale that led *los Conquistadores,* the hard-doing, hard-dying adventurers of Spain, from the plains of Kansas to the frozen wastes of *Tierra del Fuego.* They conquered Mexico, these durable men in battered, sweat-soured armor. They looted the empire of the Incas. They brought the first horses, sheep and cattle—leather, wool and transportation—to the New World. They never found *The Gilded Man*—the source of the legend that danced in the shimmering heat waves of their search—that came to flicker fitfully in the embers of their lonely fires at night. The fact that they did not find him, did not kill the myth. It slumbered down through the centuries, deep grained in the unconscious byways of men's minds.

The facts that put a golden sheen to the song that Stoddart sang were as new as Marshall's discovery in the mill race at Coloma. The Argonauts soon learned that the gold they panned where the mountain creeks and rivers reached the valley was fine as flour. As they worked upstream, the gold changed to fine sand, then coarse sand, gravel gold, slug gold and nuggets. It was easy to reach a conclusion from this sequence; somewhere in the high mountains there must be a great, solid ledge of pure metal that was *"the source of gold"* for all they found below. If a man could find this *"source of gold"* ... it would be easier pickings than wading waist deep in icy water, or packing sacks of dirt from a dry bank to the potholes that were summer's bounty. The facts, and the dream they caused, were not made overnight. They were learned the hard way as the tidal wave of '49ers crashed into California and broke against the seaport and valley towns.

Like salmon spawning, men worked their way up every trickling river, every dry creek bed, until, by autumn, they had penetrated into the foothill canyons, gashed broad and deep, great swordstrokes between the ridges, by centuries of erosion. The quest for gold, the actual taking of the precious stuff itself, submerged all thoughts of preparing for winter until Winter in all its majesty was upon them.

Rain swelled the rivers, ice filmed the sluice boxes, then clogged them, and snow blockaded the supply trails from the valley towns. The wise ones left the hills and canyons to wait for spring. The foolhardy, and the ignorant, settled down to winter tough in crude pole-and-canvas shelters, in rough shake-and-timber huts, even in brush wickiups daubed with mud. Flour was high in the hills, salt horse was higher, and whiskey was out of sight, but there was venison for camp meat and the dreams of fortune waiting in the spring to feed on when all else failed. There were spells of clear weather when a man could *"moss"* a little, even *"crevice"* if the river dropped unseasonably, to break the monotony. And to a group of men who had elected to winter on the Yuba, above Major Downie's cabins on Jersey Flat, the monotony was broken, too, when a battered fragment of humanity stumbled downstream into their camp on the Yuba's north fork.

He was a big man, gaunt and haggard, with his skin hanging in loose folds and his haunted eyes staring wildly behind a beard as matted as squaw-carpet. His clothes were brush-shredded and his boots were mockeries. Here was a mortal man on whom the wilderness had closed its jaws and the miners who gave him haven knew the signs.

They fed him sparingly from their own scant stores, easing his stomach into food. They gave him a bunk in the most weathertight habitation and nursed him with a rough gentleness during the days that followed. And they would have been less than human not to hunker around their fires discussing the derelict—who he was, whence he came, what had befallen him? They had to wait some days for the answers until the stranger's powerful frame filled out and his eyes lost their hunted look and the muscles of his neck relaxed. Then the floodgates of the stranger's tongue were opened and his story tumbled out in a cultured voice with an Old Country burr to it.

His name was Stoddart, he told them, a man who had served his time in the Royal Navy aboard the ship-of-the-line *Asia* at the battle of Acre. He had emigrated to Philadelphia when his hitch was up, and there he had prospered, first as a school teacher and then as a newspaper editor. He was a bachelor in his forty-seventh year, when President Polk's message to the Congress in December, 1848, made the rumors of Gold in California official. He had determined then and there, despite his years, to seek a golden fortune rather than one stained with printer's ink.

He had journeyed overland with a wagon train and, at the bend of the Humboldt River, he and his companions had elected to take Lassen's Cut-off, the *Emigrants Death Route to California*. They had surmounted the perils of Black Rock Desert and Massacre Valley, Fandango Pass and The Devils' Garden, to drop down the Pit and climb out again into Dixie Valley and twist across the high pine barrens to The Big Meadows. Here they had halted to recruit their livestock on the lush grass, to repair their wagons as best they could, to watch the blue-black haze of autumn creep down the slopes of Lawson's Butte, and to brace themselves for the final push over Deer Creek Pass to the great ridge that led down to California proper. While they were camped here, Stoddart and a companion, whose name he never mentioned, had gone hunting camp meat. While he did not say so, it became apparent to his listeners that nothing in Stoddart's previous life had qualified him as a woods runner or a hunter. He and his companion had gotten themselves thoroughly lost. And it should have been evident that all the country he had covered was merged into a kaleidoscope of remembered terror and confusion.

Stoddart related that he and his companion had spent several days in a fruitless effort to return to the emigrant camp in The Big Meadows. Failing in this, they had followed the essential instinct, picking out a watercourse that they felt must lead them in time to the civilization they knew was somewheres down stream and west. Using the stream as a line-of-position, they had struck out, exploring afield as the fancy took them. By Stoddart's account, they had travelled the best part of a week when they stumbled upon a little lake, some fifteen acres in extent, ringed in by shining peaks crested with new snow. They bent down to slake their thirst and as they did, their bemused brains finally told them that the rocks gleaming up at them through the crystal water were gobbets of pure gold . . . that the very sands upon which they knelt were the same stuff, only smaller. If his listeners snorted at this fable, Stoddart was unperturbed.

After taking as many samples as they could pack, more than was safe as it turned out, the two men had hurried on to meet disaster the very next day. A band of Indians jumped the two pilgrims while they were picking berries, or grubbing for roots to eat. The two men scattered like quail; his companion went his way in frantic flight and Stoddart was left alone. In the melee of his escape, Stoddart abandoned the watercourse and plunged straight across country, sliding into canyons, toiling up the other side, slogging through valleys plagued with spring holes, scrambling through tangled windfalls, just blindly bucking his way across the worst terrain in California—the headwaters of the Feather and Yuba River systems.

This was the gist of Stoddart's story, a story common to many an emigrant. Even the gold-lined lake was not incredible to Californians of '49, who had seen it proven time and time again that the very next bend of any creek held a bar much richer than the one they had left behind them. And to prove that he had found something, Stoddart showed his benefactors . . . . . nuggets!

His specimens ran from $8.00 to $25.00 apiece, soft and yellow and remarkably free from adhering mother quartz or imbedded river gravel. Stoddart's specimens had been in place where he had found them for a long, long time. They gave great credence to his story; a story that was followed promptly by Stoddart's offer to lead his saviors to the golden lake at once. It is easy to imagine the thoughts of the men who had listened to Stoddart's story—who now hefted his specimens and considered his proposition. Here was a chance to get in on the ground floor of the *"source of gold."* Here, too, was a chance to get forever wrapped in the icy shroud of death in the High Sierra and the fate of the Donner Party was still remembered in California in '49.

The fear of winter outweighed the hope of fortune so—Stoddart took his leave—saying that he was going down to San Francisco to seek word of his missing hunting partner—promising to return in the spring to lead his friends to the lake of gold. Stoddart did more than leave a promise behind him for the vision of Gold Lake started haunting the minds and dreams of men, began its psychological brain-washing, in the very wake of his going.

Not even the rigors of winter could keep the '49ers from visiting their fellows on other creeks, and bars and settlements. Stoddart's story was repeated and repeated and repeated, and it lost nothing in the tellings. Doubting Thom-asses were silenced when the teller played his clincher—Stoddart actually had shown nuggets to support his story. Other men remembered that that very summer of '49, another Gold Lake search had been organized, and the fact that it came to a sorry end was dismissed without letting it spoil the effect of compounding the truth of Stoddart's tale.

This first Gold Lake hullabaloo originated in the fertile mind of Caleb Greenwood, Old Greenwood, a mountain man and beaver trapper, who had settled down to end his days in a pleasant little valley not far from Hangtown (Placerville). Old Caleb had seen the greenhorns thrashing through the brush looking for gold and decided that he should help them. Selecting a small group, he had levied an assessment on them to defray the cost of hiring his pack mules and one of his half-breed sons for a guide; the son would guide them to the lake of which Old Greenwood knew and the pack mules would carry home the precious metal that clogged its shores. The greenhorns anted-up and the expedition sallied forth only to return in several weeks with sore feet for their trouble. When the seekers reproached Old Caleb for their misfortune, that tough nut explained it by saying that his son must have lost his way. He also denied any appeals for return of the investment with a judicious display of his Hawken rifle. This story should have spelled out a warning for Stoddart's yarn but nothing shows that it did. In fact, the yeasty ferment of Gold Lake worked its magic all that winter, finding mention in the Sacramento press by February, 1850, but it might never have borne its strange fruit if Stoddart himself had not returned to the Mother Lode country.

He did not come back to the camp on the Yuba where he had been succored but showed up in Deer Creek Dry Diggings (Nevada City), about the last week in May, 1850, still travelling solo and still retaining his specimens of water-rounded gold. The Deer Creek settlement and surrounding area was teeming with restless men, feverishly impatient for the snow pack to run off and bring the rivers down to workable levels. Stoddart told his story again, substantially as he had told it the previous fall, and he found ears ready to listen, hearts ready to believe, minds eager to pursue the chimera of Gold Lake. Men even offered Stoddart large sums of hard cash to lead them to his find but most of these he refused. He let it be known that he would take only twenty-five men, whom he would select personally from the throng of applicants, but Stoddart soon found that he was no longer master of the search for Gold Lake.

His selective attitude might have worked in the Royal Navy, or with school pupils and newspaper hirelings back in Philadelphia, but it had no place in California.

The '49ers held the firm conviction that the gold of California was created for all men to share as equally as their own abilities could manage it. If Stoddart knew of gold, he had no right to confine his knowledge to his own chosen few. That was the feeling of the times and it was expressed in action. When Stoddart led his selectmen out in the first week of June, a cloud of free riders, several hundred in number, followed after him. If he would not share his knowledge, then he would be their guide, willy-nilly, into the then unknown country that lay north of the Yuba and east of the known diggings on the Feather at Bidwell Bar.

When the news that Stoddart had started for Gold Lake rippled out across California, the town of Marysville boiled like a stirred-up ant hill. Men swarmed into it from all over the Mother Lode to outfit for the trek. The price of mules went to $400.00 a head in the town with none to be had after the first week's excitement. Marysville locals charged newcomers $100.00 a head to guide them to the trail left by Stoddart and his fellow-travellers, putting their own life up as forfeit for failing to find the sign. The newspapers, Marysville *Herald,* Sacramento *Transcript,* even the august *Alta California,* gave the Gold Lake excitement full coverage, recording among other items that the river steamer *"Governor Dana"* docked at Marysville on June 17, to find no one on the dock to greet her, let alone handle her cargo, and the town practically deserted. Even the merchants had decided to find their customers by stripping their shelves of stock, packing it on their own backs or on more expensive mules, and reaping their own golden harvest from the Gold Lakers along the trail, many of whom had started out woefully unequipped. There was pure coal oil added to the flames when the *Transcript* of June 19 printed a story about Gold Lake, made up from whole cloth, to the effect that the Indians of that region made fish hooks and arrow points from gold and had council seats carved from solid blocks of the precious metal. In fact, it seems that the *Transcript* was trying to quench the Gold Lake fever with applied hyperbole for their story went on to say that thin sheets of gold were to be found floating on the surface of the lake itself while one seeker had lassoed a boulder of the stuff beneath the lake's surface and, being unable to drag it out, had stayed with his line until he died of exhaustion. All this seems to have done was to fan the fires. Even Peter Lassen left his verdant acres in the northern valley to hike off into the hills with a group of seekers, following his own private hunch as to where Gold Lake really was. Men the length and breadth of the Mother Lode abandoned claims paying them a certain $100.00 per each and every day to stampede after the riches of Gold Lake. Before the climax came, over 1,000 men had stormed the ridges.

Stoddart took his chosen band northeast from Deer Creek Dry Diggings, across the Yuba, and up the ridge that separates the north fork of that brawling stream from the middle fork of the Feather. Turning east along the ridge spine, he went steadily on his way, every move marked by the sure confidence of a man who knows what he is doing and where he is bound. The horde of free-riders following him was hard pressed to keep his pace and the afterwave of Gold Lakers found a trail as easy to follow as the mark of a bulldozer's passage.

In just eight days time from Deer Creek Dry Diggings, Stoddart led his men off the ridge spine into Sierra Valley. It was magnificent, unknown country, with the unspoiled green reaches of the valley ringed with a diadem of crenallated, snow capped peaks. The group made camp in high satisfaction but the camp in Sierra Valley was the beginning of Stoddart's travail. His sure confidence slowly oozed away from him, then faltered abruptly, then broke apart completely. *"It's easterly a piece"* . . . *"Must be south of here . . . It's north I'm certain sure."* Finally, he did not bother to explain his changes of course, but went from one valley to another, without any signs of knowing one from the other, from one watershed to the next and back again, from ridge to ridge and stream to stream, with his followers in his wake.

His chosen twenty-five did not lose heart until the savviest among them realized that their leader was covering the same country without recognizing it. The free-riders pelting after them had nothing in their hearts but an all-consuming anger at what they conceived to be Stoddart's evasive tactics, designed to throw them off the trail, wear them down, tire them out, until they were too exhausted to make the final spurt when Stoddart stopped his wanderings and made a dash for Gold Lake with his select group. Their sentiments found expression by joining the leading twenty-five, without a by-your-leave. The whole group were together, some five hundred weary, confused, resentful men, when they camped for the night in a little meadow to the north of Sierra Valley's rolling reaches. Here the issue came to a head with Stoddart's confession that he was lost; that he could not find the lake whose sands were gobbets of pure gold.

This confirmation of their fears completed the demoralization of the Gold Lakers. Those who had abandoned paying claims to follow after Gold Lake knew what they had lost. Others had suffered the loss of their investment in mules and equipment. Still others had been fleeced by the merchants' prices for goods along the trail and ALL of them were foot-sore and heart-sick. The upshot of their frenzied arguments was the perfectly natural decision to hang the cause of their misfortune without more ado. This decision, however, was not summarily executed. The lure of Gold Lake was still strong enough to gain Stoddart one last reprieve.

A few stout hearted believers insisted that Stoddart was not crazy, only badly confused in his bump of direction. They held out for one last chance to prove that his story was not a humbug. Stoddart was informed that if the next sunset saw Gold Lake unfound, he would be strung up for the birds to roost on. The angry mob was so satisfied with their judgment and their decision, so sure that Stoddart was either crazy or confused, that they failed to post a guard over him. No matter what else Stoddart may have been, he was not crazy enough to wait around for his own hanging. That night, he "joined the birds" in his own way and when morning dawned, he was long gone. The hundreds of men who had followed him broke apart like fissioning fragments of hot rocks. If any of them did carry on a search for Gold Lake, they never found it but the finds that did come from the Gold Lake search made newspaper copy that was good reading.

San Francisco's *Alta California* ran a story over a Marysville dateline to the effect that men had come in from Gold Lake with quantities of coarse gold, and that the gravel was not only rich but was ten feet deep to bedrock. Well, the men were Gold Lakers, true enough, but the gold they had garnered came from Nelson's Point. The men said it was Gold Lake gold for a very human reason—they had been hoaxed and why admit it to the world? Another man, McClellan by name, showed up in Marysville with a poke worth $4,000.00, the results of four days' work in a pocket he struck on the back trail from Gold Lake. There were numerous other strikes, as the Gold Lakers roamed over the new country they were in, either trying to find their way out, or just stubbornly refusing to give up without something to show for their search; some of these strikes were big, some were small, and one of them was fantastic.

Three Germans, or so their nationality stands in the stories of that time, pitched out of Last Chance Valley into the canyon of the Feather River's north fork, and made their meager camp. One of them went down to the river for water next morning and the three Germans had found Rich Bar. They took out $36,000.00 in four days' work, and after them four Georgia crackers made $50,-000.00 in a single day. One pan of Rich Bar gravel netted $2,500.00 and the size of claims along Rich Bar was limited to ten square feet. In its first two years of hectic life, Rich Bar earned its name by producing better than $3,000,000.00 in fine gold, coarse gold, flake gold, slug gold, gold in nuggets, lumps and gobbets. But Crazy Stoddart got none of these riches, nor did he ever profit from the other, more enduring, wealth that stemmed from his ill-starred search.

When he left Last Chance Valley (or, as some claim, Humbug Valley), to avoid being the *piece de resistance*

105

at a hanging, Stoddart found sanctuary from Major William Downie, the braw Scot who gave his name to the town he founded on the Yuba. After his fiasco had been forgotten in the impact of Rich Bar and other strikes in the same region, Stoddart tried several times to raise other parties to find Gold Lake. But he was "Crazy" Stoddart now and, finally, he drifted down the Mother Lode to end his days in Tuolumne County—prospecting, teaching penmanship, doing ornamental writing for diplomas, and, towards the end, finding his days divested of care by the ministrations of those who had come to love him for himself.

So today, in the history of California, Thomas Robertson Stoddart has his own small niche as the man who set in motion the most dramatic demonstration of the cumulative effect of gold upon the psychology of the men who were the Argonauts. So today, a long century after he first showed those specimens of pure gold, no one has found the lake from whence he said they came. No one seems to worry about this failure either. Why should they? Along with Rich Bar and the other rich strikes they made, the Gold Lakers found other, more enduring, riches.

Some of those who followed Stoddart after Gold Lake recognized the riches in the meadow lands of Sierra, Red Clover, Mohawk, Genesee, Indian, and the other fertile valleys of the High Sierra. In many instances, their descendants still farm and ranch those lands. Other men found quartz veins and copper lodes that produced for many years; and other men in later days found minerals that served the Nation well. Still other men saw the possibilities of The Big Meadows and, today, Lake Almanor sparkles in the sun above the spot where Stoddart went out to hunt in '49 and lost his way and perhaps his mind. And Uncle Peter Lassen, foraging for Gold Lake where he thought it ought to be, was the first to see and recognize the lands around Honey Lake for what they were. So from Stoddart's will-o'-the-wisp came the first real exploration, the first real settlement, of the whole intra-montane region of Sierra, Plumas and Lassen counties, a region whose timber production has meant more cash, more solid building of California, of the Nation, than would have come from the sands of Gold Lake if they had been all they were hoped to be by those first seekers.

And today a later generation of seekers still comes to the high, clean granite wonderland between the Yuba's north fork and the middle fork of Feather River to find health of mind and body and spirit. Some seek to find these things in hiking, some in hunting, others in fishing, and some in just lazing away the golden days beside the waters of Gold Lake. There are many such with this name in the Sierra but the one that stems from the search of "Crazy" Stoddart is the mountain tarn beneath the brooding summit of Mount Elwell.

(Most printed accounts of the Gold Lake excitement refer to the principal figure as either Amos or J. R. Stoddard. The name Thomas Robertson Stoddart has been used herein on the basis of information furnished by Miss Caroline Wenzel, formerly head of the California Section of the California State Library.—W. H. H.)

Mountain Man of Color

He headed west for the last time in 1859, riding out of Westport Landing as the leaves along the Missouri bottoms turned the color of blood from a new, deep wound. He shepherded the wagons up deep-rutted tracks along the Platte that followed the trail he had helped blaze almost forty years before when he and the West were young—when the wind came down the height of land from the nameless peaks whispering *"Come and find me! Come and find me!"*

Now the weight of sixty-odd years rode with him in the saddle but he had still the look, the sweeping vision, of a scarred old cat from the rimrocks, with *"a devil-may-care expression, a face full of character and wonderful perceptive faculties; long, black hair, complexion like a Mexican and eyes like an Indian."* He was James P. Beckwourth, the most pungent of all that doughty breed who planted the American flag west of the Rockies and kept it there with the barrels of their Hawken rifles. Now, on the sunset slope of his life, Old Jim was heading for Denver to work for his old friend, Louis Vasquez. When he got to Denver, the local newspaper took him to its pages with an eager pen because Jim Beckwourth was good copy, and the bare bones of his life were readily available for flights of rhetoric in print.

The reason that Beckwourth's life was an open book was simply that he had had a book written about him. His biographer had been a peripatetic Justice of the Peace in California, Squire T. D. Bonner, of Onion Valley and adjacent areas that needed justice as he dispensed it. The only trouble was that the miners of the Feather River headwaters did not agree with Bonner on what was justice; hence, he found himself unemployed and out of funds in the winter of 1854. So—it stands in the records of Plumas County that one Joseph Davis, of Yuba City, doing business in Plumas, put up a grub-stake of $200.00 to enable Bonner to take down the personal narrative of James P. Beckwourth with a view towards publishing same and that all three parties concerned were to share in the profits of the venture.

Well, Beckwourth had a reputation of being "a bigger liar than Jim Bridger," but where Old Gabe spun his windys about phenomena of Nature, Beckwourth gave his fancy full flight about his favorite character—himself. Since Squire Bonner had no way of disproving Beckwourth's yarns, even if he had wanted to, the results made *"The Life and Times of James P. Beckwourth,"* published by Harper & Brothers in 1856, a better dime novel than most that came later in Beadles Library. By the time Jim Beckwourth hit Denver, his reputation was abroad in the land. Even if the local press, or anybody else for that matter, had been inclined to call Jim a liar, they would have had a hard time finding many of his contemporaries alive to disprove his statements.

Beckwourth had survived the Fur Trade, where the death rate among the trappers was close to 70 per cent. He had lived for almost forty years on the raw knife-edge of the frontier from the Mississippi to the Pacific when other men, just as skilled in survival, became *gone beaver.* He was smart, and he was tough, and he was lucky. He may have been part thug, and he certainly was all freebooter, but men like Colonel William Bent, Kit Carson and Ceran St. Vrain bore witness to Jim's rough honesty and sense of loyalty to his friends that were the frontier's measure of a man. And in an editorial, December 1, 1859, *The Rocky Mountain News* has this to say about Jim Beckwourth. *"We had formed the opinion, as has, we presume, almost everyone that Captain Beckwourth was a rough, illiterate, backwoodsman, but were most agreeably surprised to find him a polished gentleman, possessing a fund of general information which few can boast. He is now sixty-two years of age, but looks scarce fifty, hale, hearty and straight as an arrow."* With this welcome to Denver, Jim Beckwourth settled down to running the general store of Vasquez & Sons, and managing their stock ranch on Cherry Creek. It was something of a change of life for a man who had lived and done as had Jim Beckwourth.

He was born near Alexandria, Virginia, February 26, 1798, the son of a plantation owner, or overseer, and a quadroon woman of the plantation. The family moved to Cape Girardeau, Missouri, around 1805, and as soon as he was big enough, young Jim was apprenticed to a blacksmith named Casner in Saint Louis. Having learned the trade, Jim signed articles with General William Henry Ashley in 1823 to go to the mountains; a raw recruit in the battle between the Missouri Fur Company and the Hudsons Bay Company for the beaver lands beyond the Rockies.

In 1826, when Ashley sold out to the firm of Smith, Jackson & Sublette, Jim made a change. He had been Ashley's man, not one of Ashley's men, and the new ownership was not for him. He was no longer a greenhorn, but the equal of such hairy trappers as Jim Bridger, Hugh Glass, Jedediah Smith, Old Greenwood, Jim Clyman and the rest. He was his own master and it may have been the subtle distinction of his blood that made him restless among the Kentucky and Tennessee stock who predominated west of the Front Range peaks. Whatever the reason, Beckwourth packed his traps and his possibles on his horses and cut stick for the Sparrowhawk People, whose land along the headwaters of Powder River was rich in beaver and chances to fight.

Now it was one thing to get an Indian wife but another thing to really join an Indian tribe. Jim Beckwourth rode into the Crow village, as cool as a beaver trap in winter, and made his play and made it stick. Trading on his coloration, Jim swore that he was a Crow by birth, stolen when a baby by enemies and traded to the white man. Now he had returned to join his people. The Crows believed him. Jim was a past master of Indian psychology even then, and they had no cause to regret the prodigal's return.

Jim knew the white man's wiles with alcohol—how 40 gallons of raw spirits made 1,600 pints of trade whiskey— popskull—each pint demanding a tanned buffalo hide in purchase. The Crows laid off firewater in favor of

110

useful things like powder and ball and flints and traps and knives and finery for their horses and their women. When it came to warfare, the swart, muscular body of Jim Beckwourth, a blacksmith trained and a Mountain Man raised, cost the Blackfoot many scalps and his prowess earned him an honored name, The Bloody Arm. When it came to horse stealing, Jim could raid a Comanche horse herd as easily as he drew breath and anyone who could steal horses from the Comanche was a past master of the art. When the American Fur Company of John Jacob Astor opened a trading post among the Blackfoot, traditional enemies of the Crows, Jim got himself made Astor's agent among his adopted people to see that they got a fair shake with the gun supply. In short, the Crows were a great people as long as Jim Beckwourth lived with them and that was a good ten years.

In 1837, Jim apparently got tired of being a demigod among the Crows. He went to the white man's war against Seminole Indians in Florida, serving as a scout under General Jessup. The Army lists do not show his name during the fracas but this is no sign that he did not serve as he said he did. He joined a Volunteer Regiment from Saint Louis and volunteer outfits in those days were notorious for lack of records. Jim did draw the long-bow many times but never as to where he had been; just as to what he had done.

After the Seminole trouble, Jim did not return to the Crows. The beaver trade was played out and Jim's restlessness led him Southwest, to New Mexico and adjoining Utah. Here he turned to a form of practical land piracy. He and Peg-Leg Smith, another ex-Mountain Man, took a war party of Utes and hit for California over the Mojave Desert and Cajon Pass. According to the most credible account of this foray, Jim went ahead to spy out the land, staying at *Rancho Del Chino* in the guise of a trapper, until he knew the location of every *remuda* in the region. Then Peg-Leg and the Utes came down to join them and when they headed east again, they drove some 3,000 *Californio* horses with them.

111

The proceeds from this raid set Beckwourth up in business in Taos, New Mexico. Here he wooed, won and actually wed Senorita Luisa Sandeville and at the age of 43 it seemed that maybe Jim would settle down. He might have had it not been for politics. And for once, they were none of his choosing or causing.

The Texas filibustering expedition of 1841 scared New Mexico's officialdom out of their *serapes*. Even though they captured the Texans and sent them down the Rio Grande Valley to Chihuahua, lopping off the ears of those that died on the way to show none escaped, they were jittery about all *Yanquis*, no matter what color skin they had. Beckwourth went out of business; took what he could salvage, including his horses and his new wed wife, and headed for Colorado.

Where Fountain Creek flowed into the Arkansas, Jim made his camp. That this camp would grow into Pueblo, Colorado; that there was untold wealth in coal all around him, were unknown facts to Jim Beckwourth. He hunted meat for Bent's Fort and later in the year, 1842, he moved up to the *Cache la Poudre,* near Greeley today, where he traded for the brothers, St. Vrain. Here he met John Charles Fremont, starting his education and his publicity campaign in the West, and Fremont noted in his diary that they "concocted a very good julep from wild mint." Even though Fremont was a fire-eating South Carolinian, he seems to have met and drunk with Jim Beckwourth, the mulatto, on terms of complete equality. Fremont may have been guided by his scouts— Lucien Maxwell and Kit Carson—who knew that Jim Beckwourth was more man than most.

Sometime in the next two years, Jim and his wedded wife parted company. He showed up alone in Los Angeles in 1844, this time as a peaceful trader and he apparently did well and kept his hands off other folk's horses. By Jim's own account, he raised a company of fellow-Americans in 1844 to support the revolt of Don Jose Castro against the Governor, Micheltorena, who had John Sutter's Foreign Legion of American riflemen for firepower. Bancroft's *History of California* does support Jim's claim that he was with Castro, although it does not corroborate Jim's own account of his own importance in that relatively bloodless revolution. After this affair had been settled, Jim went back to his trading business in Los Angeles until the Bear Flag Revolt merged into the War With Mexico.

By Jim's own account, he took 1,800 horses and mules out of California in the summer of 1846 without benefit of bill of sale. He drove his catch back to Pueblo, Colorado, where he sold them to defray the costs of patriotism. He filled in the rest of the war by carrying military dispatches between Santa Fe, New Mexico and Fort Leavenworth; on one trip covering the almost 950 miles in fifteen days, which is not bad for a man nearing fifty years of age.

Jim came back again to California in 1848, carrying dispatches and, this time, he foreswore horse theft. Times had changed in California. It had never been a crime to raid the *Californios* but, now, California was United States soil, filled with his fellow-countrymen who had a direct sense of applied justice—a long rope and a fast drop. He carried mail and dispatches between Monterey and Captain Dana's ranch at Nipomo for a living and, by his own account, he led a group of Vigilantes who meted out summary justice to the murderers of the Reed family near San Miguel.

When the big rush of '49 hit California, Jim went to Sonora and into the clothing and saloon business. He knew there were easier ways to make a stake than grubbing in the gravel bars. He prospered but evidently he could not withstand the epidemic of Gold Lake Fever that swept the Mother Lode in 1850. Like all the others who followed "Crazy" Stoddart to search for the fabulous lake whose beaches were made of nuggets only, Jim did not find it. Nor did he, like others of the disappointed searchers, make a strike like Rich Bar. However, he did get into American Valley on this trip, going from there across country to Pit River and down it to Old Shasta. It was on this trip, by Jim's account, that he suspected the existence of the Pass that bears his name today.

The next spring, 1851, Jim came back to American Valley, bought a steer from Mr. Turner, and headed east into Sierra Valley and onwards to Beckwourth Pass, the lowest breach in the sheer eastern wall of the Sierra Nevada. Jim had not been a Mountain Man for nothing. He knew terrain and what it meant to ox and mule power. This Pass and the valleys that lay west of it made a far easier route into California than did either the Carson, Donner or Henness gateways then in use. And Jim Beckwourth knew, too, what such a route could mean to the California town where it terminated in the deep valley of the Sacramento. Jim rode down to Marysville and said his say.

The Mayor, S. M. Miles, and other substantial citizens were enthusiastic. The road that Jim proposed would lead the emigrant traffic right to Marysville without filtering it through other communities first. A popular subscription was opened to defray construction costs and Jim hot-footed it back to the mountains to turn the tide of emigration over Beckwourth Pass. He was too late for the 1851 travel but next spring his road left Truckee Meadows near present Glendale, Nevada, following generally the line of US Highway 395 to the Pass, thence across Sierra Valley to the Middle Fork of Feather River and down the dividing ridge to Marysville. The first wagon train that used this route was enthusiastic about its easy grades and the good feed en route. In this train was a girl of eleven years who rode into California sitting in front of Jim Beckwourth on his barebacked horse, with his arm holding her steady. Telling of this event seventy-five years later, on April 24, 1927, Ina Coolbrith, California's first poet laureate, said Jim Beckwourth was *"to my mind one of the most beautiful creatures that ever lived."* Handsome is as handsome does, they say, and Jim had done handsomely on his own hook because the subscription that was being raised in Marysville to pay for the road fell flat and Jim, by his own reckoning, was out of pocket some $1,600 for road work. Still, he had a lucrative business trading and guiding for the emigrants who used his road into California.

Jim's cabin stood on a hillside about two and one-half miles west of the town of Beckwourth today, the site of the Alexander Kirby residence later. A second cabin was soon built by Jim as his business expanded but both were burned and he built a third log house that served as his trading-post and hotel. And in Jim's words, as Squire Bonner wrote them down: *"Here is a valley 240 miles in circumference containing the choicest land in the world. Its yeild of hay is incalculable; the red and white clovers spring up simultaneously, and the grass that covers its smooth surface is of the most nutritive nature. And springs flow as pure as any that refresh this verdant earth."* The passage of a century since Jim Beckwourth raised the first walls in that valley has proved that he didn't lie about it.

Why Jim left his trading post, hotel and fertile valley after the winter of 1854-55 is clothed in obscurity. The local legends have it that when the emigrant trade over his Pass slacked off, Jim's old sense of property rights asserted itself and a group of locals asked him to leave, and to leave their four-footed property where it belonged. Jim showed up in New Mexico, around Santa Fe and Taos, in 1857, and by 1858 had gone east to Saint Louis, whence in 1859, he rode west again, on the beginning of that trail where all pony tracks point just one way.

Jim's last years in Denver seem almost an anticlimax. He ran the Vasquez store and managed their stock ranch as related. He married Miss Elizabeth Lettbetter in 1860, and in 1861, he went ranching for himself on the South Platte below Denver, trapping what beaver still lived in the streams about him for pocket money. Jim managed to keep out of the newspapers and the history books until 1864.

In the spring of this year, Jim applied for a commission as Captain in a Regiment of Colorado Volunteers then being organized but didn't make the riffle. In August of this year, a local tough who rejoiced in the name of "Nigger Bill" made the mistake of choosing Old Jim Beckwourth and the Denver paper duly states that Jim was acquitted on the valid plea of self-defense.

He might be sixty-six years old but he could still take care of James P. Beckwourth.

This, then, is the scant record of his pastoral years. The retirement of the warrior to prosaic farming while the shadows of the mountains seemed to grow longer with each season. The old days were long ago and far away and Jim Beckwourth had his memories to warm his heart. What memories they must have been — *the sight and sound and smell of a Crow village on the move—the caress of sunset on lands he was first to see and travel—the times he'd had and the wine he'd taken and great herds of stolen horses raising a dust half-way across a continent.* All these things could come flooding back to him while far to the East the Confederate States thrashed in their death agony. In this same fall, west of the Mississippi, there was blood on the plains as Cheyenne, Arapaho, Kiowa and Comanche cut the stage lines that linked Colorado to the Nation. The old man smelled the smoke of battle and saddled up to ride with Colonel Chivington.

The command left Fort Lyon after dark on November 28, 1864, with a biting wind out of the north and the stars glinting frostily in the night. It was hard lines for old bones and Jim Beckwourth was almost numb in the saddle as he scouted ahead of the Third Colorado Cavalry for the hostiles' camp on Sand Creek. He found it, and Chivington's 700 Volunteers hit Black Kettle's people at sunrise on November 29. The surprise was complete and when the fight was over, some 400 Cheyenne, men, women and children, were witness to the fact that it was easy for the white man to be just as barbarous in war as ever the Cheyenne had been. Jim settled down on his little ranch after Sand Creek, keeping his own counsel but having nothing more to do with the local militia. Even as he pottered about his beaver traps and his garden, events were shaping up in the country he once had known that would enable him to perform another service to his country.

The gold strike in Last Chance Gulch in Montana suddenly became of national importance, since it could help pay off the debts of the Civil War. So, in violation of a solemn treaty with the Sioux, Colonel Henry B. Carrington moved his Regulars out of Fort Laramie on June 17, 1866, to open a road to the Montana goldfields around the Big Horn Mountains, the heartland of the Sioux and the country of Beckwourth's old friends, the Crow. Carrington's job was not easy. Red Cloud, the fighting Oglala, "stood in the way" and between the forts that Carrington built, Fetterman, Reno, Phil Kearny and C. F. Smith, the white man's road, The Bozeman Trail, belonged to the Sioux. As the broiling summer wore on, the harassed Colonel Carrington heard of worse troubles building up. Rumors came out of the vast, silent, sea of grass around him that the Sioux were propositioning the Crow to join forces against the white man. Carrington had troubles enough without adding Crow warriors to his list. He took counsel with Jim Bridger, and be it to Carrington's credit that he took Bridger's advice which is more than most Regular Army officers ever deigned to do with civilian scouts.

Bridger's advice to the Colonel was short and to the point—"*Get thet damned lyar Jim Beckwourth to make medicine with the Crow.*" The word came down the miles to Old Jim on his ranch and he took the trail again to see the people he had not seen for almost thirty years since he went off to fight the Seminoles in Florida. In the records of the War Department it stands that "*James P. Beckwourth was employed as a scout and guide at Fort Laramie, Dakota Territory, from 1 August to 13 August, 1866, at the rate of $75.00 a month; and from 13 August to 31 August, 1866, he was employed in Montana and in the field as a scout and guide at the rate of $5.00 a day.*"

At Fort Laramie, Jim gave Seth Ward a note for $93.70, payment for a bill of goods to take as presents to the Crow, the people to whom he had given great victories and strong medicine as long as he had lived with them. Then Old Jim rode off into the rolling, tawny prairies of the Wind River country and, in time, the word came back to Colonel Carrington that the Crow would not join the Sioux against the white man. In fact,

117

the Crow were enthusiastic about joining the white man against the Sioux. But Beckwourth did not come back himself. He stayed with the Crow people. Permanently!

Some stories have it that Jim just died of old age among the people who had adopted him so many years before. The other story, which the Crow themselves confirm, is that they deliberately poisoned Jim Beckwourth, because: *"He was our good medicine. We had been more successful under him than under any chief. If we could not have him living, it would be good medicine to have him with us dead."*

It may seem in this day and age that Jim Beckwourth was not a genteel person but he cannot be judged by the conventions of a house-dwelling society. He was a carnivore in a day and age when vegetarians either died young or went back East for good. He was a Mountain Man, of whom Frank Waters wrote these words: *"Where they went no man is certain save that of all men who ever lived, none were given to span such horizons. Unknown rivers ran in their blood, fury made home in their hearts, and a vast loneliness that even the Rockies could not fill engulfed them forever. Their lives are like the winds that sweep down the canyons; you can hear the voices but can find no footprints."*

And yet Jim Beckwourth left not footprints but his name upon the land he loved—Beckwourth Pass where a railroad and a highway breach the range throughout the year—Beckwourth Peak and Beckwourth Valley and the town of that same name. More, a log cabin stands above State Highway 24, mercifully spared by the cut that eased the grade. It is a tool shed now for Guido Ramelli. It stands as proof that no matter what else Jim Beckwourth did, he did good work with his hands.

Lost Mine on Your Doorstep

The legend of Peter Lassen's Lost Mine is as old as the first white settlement he made in the valley north of New Helvetia—*Bosquejo,* The Wooded Place—where Deer Creek breaks from the hills to cross the Vina Plains and reach the rolling Sacramento. The legend of Obe Leininger's Ledge is a little younger for Obe Leininger was a seeker after the Lost Mine whose stories had been part and parcel of his youth—the tales told around the hearth of a winter evening in the days before good roads, radio, television and picture magazines.

The foothill Indians of that region, the Yahi, gained an evil reputation amongst the early settlers for their acquired taste for ox and mule meat, for their skill at homicide and evasive tactics. Yet these same Indians, when opportunity afforded, were wont to bring in coarse gold to trade at the settlements of Hall's Ferry (Tehama), Monroeville, and other river towns long since gathered into the sea. Since Peter Lassen treated these people as people, not as vermin, he was reputed to know and use their secret trove. Moreover, in 1850, an educated emigrant, J. Goldsborough Bruff, who was surveying a town site for Lassen and "General" John Wilson, made certain entries in his diary: *"June 18* In the afternoon Lassen and Dexter started out for the hills a short distance: *July 2* At daybreak Lassen and Dexter returned . . . . . Lassen had some *fine samples of gold he found."* This same diarist noted, also, that when Lassen was robbed by an emigrant he had befriended, they had to weigh the dust on recovery to see if Uncle Peter had gotten back all that he had lost.

So the stories of Lassen's private gold supply flourished during the years he lived in the valley and after. That Lassen was forever in financial difficulties, that he died, far out in the Black Rock Desert of Nevada, seeking the Lost Hardin Mine, and still not wealthy—these

119

facts were not enough to still the legend. Facts never are if the legend speaks of deep human hopes.

The legend gained a new lease on life almost twenty years after Lassen's death in 1859, when little spits of snow hissed against the brush in Deer Creek canyon and swirled into the eyes of Obe Leininger as he swung up his miner's pick and buried it deep in the trunk of the tree beside him. This was his way of marking the ledge of gold-flecked quartz he had just found against the day when he could return and stake his claim according to law. He could not stay in the moment of success lest the snow block him and his partner in until their scant provisions were exhausted.

Whether Obe Leininger found Lassen's Lost Mine or made a new find for himself is immaterial. What matters these days is simply that Leininger's Ledge is truly a lost mine on your doorstep, as close as the ignition switch in the family car and the freedom of vacation time.

You can base your search at a Forest Service campground beside the cold, clear crystal waters of one of California's better trout streams. You reach this haven, or go out for supplies after you get there, over State Highway 32, amidst magnificent Sierran scenery. If this sounds remarkably like the pre-election promises of an aspiring candidate, the best way to disprove it is to see for yourself.

State Highway 32 lifts you out of the Sacramento Valley at Chico by one of the most spectacular, ridge-spine ascents in all the foothills. The highway follows, generally, the course of the Humboldt Road, an artery of commerce between California and southwestern Idaho in the Sixties, to Forest Ranch and on to Lomo where the Humboldt Road goes right to the summer homes of heat-sick valley residents at Butte Meadows and Jonesville.

Your road, State Highway 32, swings left at Lomo, snaking around the canyons and ridge ends that feed Big Chico creek, until it crosses the Deer Creek watershed and descends past Windy Cut, where it is good manners to stop at the Ranger Station to register and get a Fire

Permit. Below Windy Cut, the highway crosses Deer Creek by a bright, silvery bridge and a matter of a mile more brings you to the Potato Patch campground— stoves, tables, water faucets and wood for the cutting. There are other Forest Service camps in Deer Creek canyon but Potato Patch is best for your purposes. Your distance from Chico is a long forty miles; your distance from supplies, Auto Club services and hot-and-cold indoor conveniences is a scant thirty miles to Mineral, gateway to Lassen National Park, or to Chester and Lake Almanor. You can get on the ground quicker and easier than did Obe Leininger.

Leininger came back to the Vina Plains where he had been reared, from working in the Montana mines. His brother, John Leininger, was ranching there and after his homecoming had been accomplished, Obe Leininger decided to exercise the daemon that had long ridden him by looking for Peter Lassen's Lost Mine. He propositioned a neighboring rancher to side him in the search but this man, too, was busy with the jobs of running a ranch and feeding a family—the responsibilities of marriage and land left no time for feckless wayfaring. Obe Leininger and another bachelor, Spence Brown, were the two who set out with one pack-horse, *Johnnie*, up the old Lassen Trail out of the valley along the great ridge that separates the canyons of Deer Creek and Mill Creek. They worked their way well up the ridge, into the stand of ponderosa called Lassen's Pinery, making their headquarters at what was known to them as Lost Camp.

It took them several days to prospect the precipitous slopes running down from Lost Camp towards the canyon. Then, plunging into the gore of the canyon itself, above the deep indentation called Wilson's Cove, they found a great ledge of gold-bearing quartz where two small ravines forked. They built location markers of loose boulders and with the snow making an unmistakable threat, Obe Leininger drove his pick into the nearest tree and he and Spence Brown started to get out.

They did not know that they were lost until nightfall, when they realized they were stepping in their own boot-tracks. Next day, they tried again, rimming out of the canyon by main strength and blind instinct, until they came upon a familiar landmark, a rock in the form of a figure 4, that marked a trail into Deer Creek canyon from what they knew as Obe Field's Camp on the Lassen Trail. From this landmark, they found their own camp handily enough, fed *Johnnie* a bait of oak leaves and headed down the trail for the Vina Plains and home.

They spent one night on their way back at the ranch of Thomas Benton Polk, the man Obe had asked to side him on the search. One of the Polk youngsters, Martin, remembers Obe Leininger chaffing his father for not coming with him and Martin Polk remembers, too, the specimens that he saw in Obe Leininger's hands in the mellow, yellow lamplight of long ago. "Good rock," Leininger called them, and he never made any other claim for the ledge he found and lost save this—"Good rock!" But Martin Collins Polk, trained engineer, long-time Assessor of Butte County, familiar spirit of mines real and mines imaginary in all the northern Sierra, has himself found evidence that Obe Leininger was not lying about the quartz ledge in Deer Creek canyon, even though Obe Leininger could never find his ledge again.

This came about in 1907 when Martin was bucking the Oro Light & Power Company for a water right in Deer Creek canyon. Running a flume-line grade upstream from his family's summer grazing homestead at Polk Springs, Martin found his head-gate site to be at the mouth of Calf Creek, just half a mile below the silvery bridge that carries State Highway 32 across Deer Creek below Windy Cut today. Here, he found quartz float. He does not say that it was shot with stringers, heavy with gold—he is too honest to salt himself—but it was promising.

However, Martin was then too intent upon the latent wealth in the waters of Deer Creek to follow up his float. Today, forty-seven years later, Martin Polk is still too busy to go a'seeking after Leininger's Ledge. Someday, perhaps, when he really retires, he may look on the side-hill to the left of State Highway 32, between the mouth of Calf Creek and Potato Patch campground. Somewheres in there should be the ledge that spawned the float he found so many years ago. Perhaps the same ledge that loaded the gravel sluiced out by the Jackson and Occidental mines in Deer Creek canyon in the middle-eighties. *Quien Sabe?*

In all the years that have passed since that snow-spitting day, no one has yet found the quartz ledge beneath the pick-marked tree. A resident of Los Angeles, Mr. C. F. Carlson, spent twenty summers seeking Leininger's Ledge and never found it. Standing on the butt end of a ridge, where the Campbellville Lookout perches, a logger named Laurence Blunkall has looked out across the Devil's Den to Wilson's Cove and the whole tangled complex of Deer Creek drainage and knows that his father found the pick-marked tree in there *somewheres.* His father was riding for cattle in that country, a newcomer he was and did not know the local legends including the significance of that pick-marked tree, and when he had learned them he could never go back to it again.

And once when Martin Polk was serving Chico as City Engineer, a stranger came to his office one fine morning and requested Martin's help. The man had found Obe Leininger's ledge, so Martin heard him say, while on a hiking trip in Deer Creek, and he needed Martin's knowledge to locate it properly. He had the geology of the canyon down pat; he had the geography of the canyon down pat; every question Martin asked him brought a reasonable answer. Martin Polk's interest increased accordingly until the lucky finder remarked that it was only by luck that he had spotted the pick, because in the years that had passed since Obe Leininger drove it there, the tree in growing had carried the pick up many, many feet into the air. Martin then decided that he was too busy to go wandering around Deer Creek canyon with a man who did not know that trees grow from the top up, not the bottom.

So, Leininger's Ledge and Lassen's Lost Mine, be they the same or different, are still where their finders left them—handy to the highway, to clear mountain water, and to trout. If you seek them in vain, it may be that the search will bring you other and more lasting values. It has done so to at least one seeker who is unnamed here.

THE WINE OF THE COUNTRY

When Isaac Roop went over the mountains from Shasta, to restore his shattered fortunes and to take up land that was so rich in natural humus it would "mire a saddle blanket," he traded with the emigrants and he kept a register in his log cabin above the banks of Susan River.

In this register, emigrants could note their safe arrival thus far on the westward trek. They could leave messages for friends behind them on the trail; together with their uninhibited comments on the journey.

In this register, too, the little group of Never Sweats could enter their comments on life as they found it in Honey Lake Valley. Here is one such entry from Isaac Roop's register:

ROOP HOUSE—Sunday Aug 31st. (1856)
"Another Sabbath has passed on the swift pinions of Time, and we are one week nearer eternity. A few years more and we shall have passed smoothly down the stream of Life and paid the debt of Nature. How different then will this far famed Elysian valley appear. Where now stands Lassen's log cabin, a modern pig sty will have been erected and round that sage covered ranch will be a rail-worm fence composed chiefly of piles of brush. Who among this generation will be able to recognize this valley? Echo answers: "nary bugger."

⁂   *   *   *

One of the first men ever elected to the office of Justice of the Peace in Tehama, the booming stage center and freighting community, was William Brown Ide, one time President of the Bear Flag Republic.

Now Tehama County at that time was attached to an adjoining county for purposes of judicial processes which complicated Ide's task but did not interfere with his dispensation of justice.

Shortly after he assumed office, an alleged horse thief was haled before Justice Ide. The weather was bad, the roads were worse, and the nearest for-hire attorney was in Oroville. The county attorney was an even more distant figure, Colusa way. If there was to be a fair trial, it was squarely up to Ide.

Justice Ide asked the defendant if he had any objections to his (Ide's) appearing as attorney-for-the-defense. The alleged horse thief wanted an attorney, so he accepted Ide's offer. Ide thereupon proceeded to act as defense attorney, prosecuting attorney and judge.

In his capacity as attorney, both of them, Ide made motions and offered objections thereto; then he argued pro and con on said motions and objections; finally, he ruled upon said motions and objections.

He examined witnesses for the defense and witnesses for the prosecution and ruled as to the admissability of their evidence. He made arguments for and against the prisoner, who may have been a little bewildered by this time, and he summed up each side of the case and rebutted it in turn.

Finally, in his extreme judicial capacity, Ide summoned the prisoner to appear before the bar of justice.

"You have been defended by able counsel," said Judge Ide, "who has protected your every interest. I pronounce you Guilty, as charged."

*   *   *   *   *

The Honorable Moses Bean, first county judge of Butte County, was as confirmed in his own judgments as was his later, and more famous, Texas namesake, Roy Bean—The Law West of the Pecos.

It is recounted that Bean of Butte once handed down a judgment that suffered reversal on appeal to a higher court. Shortly after this *contretemps,* a very similar case came before His Honor.

Judge Bean staunchly handed down a judgment that followed his previous pronouncement, the one that had been overturned by the higher court.

The attorney who stood to lose by this steadfastness sprang to his feet, not wishing to undergo the labor of an appeal, and reminded His Honor that in the previous case, almost identical with this one now before the bar, his judgment had been set aside, even reversed by the higher court. *Therefore and whereas,* the judgment of the higher court in the proceeding case should be accepted as the law and the precedent in this case.

Judge Bean heard the attorney through with a most judicial silence. Then he ruled on the argument:

"If the superior courts of this state see proper to make fools of themselves, that is no reason this court should. Mr. Clerk, enter up the judgment."

OUR BOOKS

Our books make great gifts and additions to any library. Please contact us to order any of our titles. Sales of these books support our mission to promote research and publish additional titles about local history.

The Road to Cherokee
Mary Ray King, 2016, 400 pp. $24.95

The Lassen Peak Eruptions & Their Lingering Legacy
Alan Willendrup, 2015, 112 pp. $19.95

Tales of Ishi Country
Gene Serr, editor, 2012, 102 pp. $21

The Oroville-Quincy Ridge Route
David Brown, 2012, 132 pp. $21

John Bidwell: The Adventurous Life of a California Pioneer
Nancy Leek, 2010, 118 pp. $20

In Search of Captain Warner
Pat Barry, 2011, 66 pp. $20

A History of Hutchinson Lumber Company, Oroville, California
Jonathan Patrick Barnes, 1997, 89 pp. $9.75

A Historical Geography, Analysis of the Modoc Indian War
Gregory A. Reed, 1994, 121 pp. $8.50

From the Prairie to the Pacific: A Trip with Covered Wagon and Oxen Team in 1853
Henrietta Catherine Furnell, 2005, 104 pp. $8

George Moses Gray—His Reminiscences of the Life and Times of John Bidwell
Paul Roberts, editor, 1999, 64 pp. $8.50

John Brown's Family in Red Bluff, 1864-1870
Wilbert L. Phay, 1986, 66 pp. $6.50

Old Days in Butte
Florence Danforth Boyle, 2006, 172 pp. $24